A

-Substance Book

Many of the [...] philosophers [...] aestheticians [...] music [...] to. poetry in their Analysis of the possibility or impossibility of image having a representative quality or aspect.

The Composer's Voice

THE
COMPOSER'S
VOICE

Edward T. Cone

University of California Press
Berkeley • Los Angeles • London

UNIVERSITY OF CALIFORNIA PRESS
BERKELEY AND LOS ANGELES, CALIFORNIA

UNIVERSITY OF CALIFORNIA PRESS, LTD.
LONDON, ENGLAND

COPYRIGHT © 1974, BY
THE REGENTS OF THE UNIVERSITY OF CALIFORNIA

ISBN: 0–520–02508–3
LIBRARY OF CONGRESS CATALOG CARD NUMBER: 73–80830

PRINTED IN THE UNITED STATES OF AMERICA

The Ernest Bloch Professorship of Music and the Ernest Bloch Lectures were established at the University of California in 1962 in order to bring distinguished figures in music to the Berkeley campus from time to time. Made possible by the Jacob and Rosa Stern Musical Fund, the professorship was founded in memory of Ernest Bloch (1880–1959), Professor of Music at Berkeley from 1940 to 1959.

THE ERNEST BLOCH PROFESSORS

1964	RALPH KIRKPATRICK
1965–66	WINTON DEAN
1966–67	ROGER SESSIONS
1968–69	GERALD ABRAHAM
1971	LEONARD B. MEYER
1972	EDWARD T. CONE

Contents

Preface

This book presents, in revised form, the substance of six public lectures I delivered during the spring of 1972 as Ernest Bloch Professor of Music at the University of California, Berkeley. I am grateful to the Music Department there, and to the Jacob and Rosa Stern Musical Fund, for giving me the opportunity of trying out my ideas on an informed and stimulating audience; the final form of those ideas, as presented in what follows, owes much to my discussions with members of that audience. In particular, I should like to thank the following for their criticisms and suggestions: Professors William J. Bouwsma, Alan Curtis, Daniel Heartz, and Andrew Imbrie; Mr. Brad Robinson; and Mrs. J. R. Levenson. Professor George Pitcher, of Princeton University, after convincing me that what I am trying to do lies at least partially within the field of philosophy, read through the entire manuscript from that point of view. His comments were most helpful, and if a number of errors in that area still remain, they are due to my own stubbornness.

I should like to offer a final acknowledgment by quoting my original dedication of the lectures:

It is a source of great pleasure and pride for me to be here under these auspices. I was privileged to meet Ernest Bloch only once, but that once was a terrifying and exhilarating experience that I shall never forget. But a much more important connection links me with Bloch. Through his pupil, Roger Sessions, he became a sort of musical grandfather to me; and indirectly I received from him invaluable contributions to my own musical education. So it is with a real sense of a long-standing debt repaid that I dedicate these essays to his memory.

Edward T. Cone

1

Some Thoughts on "Erlkönig"

Music is a language. Such, at least, is the implicit assumption, if not the explicit assertion, of many of those who talk and write about it. Music communicates, it makes statements, it conveys messages, it expresses emotions. It has its own syntax, its own rhetoric, even its own semantics. For we are told that music has meaning, although no two authorities seem able to agree on what that meaning is. There is consequently a great deal of discussion concerning just what music says and how, indeed, it can say anything. But in all this argument one question is seldom, if ever, asked: If music is a language, then who is speaking?

This is not a trivial question, nor is it satisfied by the trivial answer, "the composer." In order to make this clear, let me ask an analogous question in the domain of literature: Who is speaking in a poem or in a work of fiction? Aristotle suggested one set of answers when he pointed out a difference between three forms of poetry that roughly correspond to what we now call the lyric, dramatic, and narrative (for example, epic) modes. In the lyric, the poet speaks in his own voice; in the drama, he speaks only through the voices of his characters; in the narrative, he combines both techniques.[1] T. S. Eliot, in a well-known essay,[2] put the triple division in another way: the poet talking to himself (as in many lyrics), addressing an audience (as in epic recitation), and assuming the role of a character (as in a play). But some critics wonder whether the poet

[1] *Poetics*, 3.
[2] *The Three Voices of Poetry* (London: Cambridge University Press, 1953).

ever really speaks in his own voice. They suggest that he is always assuming a role—a persona, as it is now fashionable to call it—even when that persona is an implied version of the poet himself.[3] It is easy to accept this principle as applying to such a poem as "Lycidas," for the shepherd-poet of pastoral convention is obviously a persona and has long been accepted as one. But those who hold the all-inclusive view insist that the Keats who speaks to us in the "Ode to a Nightingale" is equally a persona. Despite their resemblances, the Keats of the poem is no more to be identified with John Keats the poet than the shepherd of "Lycidas" with the historical John Milton.

Prose fiction, too, according to this theory, is narrated not by the author directly but by his persona, who may or may not be a character in the story. Even when the author insists that he is talking to us in his own person we must not believe him; else we shall fall into the traps laid by the real Marcel Proust for those who try to identify him with the fictional Marcel, or with the supposed author pretending to write the autobiography of the fictional Marcel.[4]

The hypothesis underlying this point of view is an appealing one: that a basic act of dramatic impersonation underlies all poetry, all fiction, indeed all literature worth the name. Perhaps it is the presence of this element that distinguishes literature as an art, setting it off from other modes of writing. Be that as it may, it saves the lyric poet who consciously exploits it from falling into maudlin sentimentality, and it prevents the reader who recognizes it from naively interpreting any poem as simple autobiography. If an analogous element could be established as

[3] See, for example, Laurence Perrine, *Sound and Sense* (New York: Harcourt, Brace and World, 1956), p. 21.

[4] See Wayne C. Booth, *The Rhetoric of Fiction* (Chicago: University of Chicago Press, 1961). I am greatly indebted to this seminal study, which throws brilliant light on problems of literary technique that are in many respects analogous to the musical questions I shall be attempting to deal with.

functioning in musical composition, it would save us from the kind of oversimplification that detects obvious suicidal intentions in Tchaikovsky's Sixth Symphony and premonitions of bereavement in the *Kindertotenlieder*; it could be used to develop an explanation of Beethoven's ability to write triumphantly affirmative music in the face of personal disaster; and it might also prove a tool for examining such concepts as the alleged insincerity of Liszt's music and the simple piety that is supposed to shine through Bruckner's.

In a wider context, one might say that the expressive power of every art depends on the communication of a certain kind of experience, and that each art in its own way projects the illusion of the existence of a personal subject through whose consciousness that experience is made known to the rest of us. That is the role of the character in a play, of the narrator in a novel, of the persona in a lyric. A picture implies the presence of an observer —the artist's persona, if you like—whose point of view we are invited to share. Similarly, an observing persona may be thought of as walking around a free-standing statue, so as to see all sides of it, whereas he walks not only around but through a building. In the case of the cinema, those of us who think of it as an independent art rather than as a branch of drama find its controlling consciousness in the moving eye of the camera (rather than in the characters that it records).[5] But what is the analogous experiencing subject in the case of music?

When the question is put in this form, it is clear that its importance does not depend on the metaphor of music as language, which, although illuminating in some respects, is still only a metaphor. It is by no means the only useful one, or necessarily the most appropriate. But whether music is considered as a language, or as many languages, or as a medium for some other

[5] See Suzanne Langer, "A Note on Film" in *Feeling and Form* (New York: Scribner's, 1953), pp. 411–416.

3

type of utterance, or as a pattern of gestures, or as a vehicle for any other form of purposive activity, the same question arises: who is to be conceived as responsible for the activity?

Despite the analogies I have implied between the musical and literary arts, it would be idle to search for "voices" in music that exactly parallel those of imaginative literature. Chopin's nocturnes are sometimes called "lyrics" and his ballades "narratives," but only by virtue of imprecisely suggestive comparison. "Dramatic," on the other hand, is applied literally to music for the stage; but it, too, is often used figuratively to characterize music (for example, Beethoven's symphonies) felt to express conflict, suspense, and resolution. In any event, these are hardly useful categories by which to classify musical forms or styles.

At the same time, there is something oddly suggestive about Eliot's three voices if they are applied, not to types of composition, but to modes of performance. For it is roughly true that music, according to its character, can variously imply the performer talking to himself, addressing an audience, or assuming the role of a personage. That is to say, some music is written primarily for the players' own enjoyment, the presence or absence of others being irrelevant. Some music is obviously designed for performance before audiences, whether in church or concert hall. Just as obviously, opera, oratorio, and other forms of vocal music require singers to impersonate dramatic characters. These divisions are by no means hard and fast. Piano four-hand music, for which intimate performance seems most appropriate, can nevertheless tolerate an audience; and one can play a piece designed for virtuoso display, like a Liszt concert-etude, for one's own enjoyment. Many operas at times seem to allow their actors to step out of their roles and sing directly to the audience. (Indeed, the Prologue to *Pagliacci* demands this effect.)

4

What I wish to suggest is something more fundamental: that all music, like all literature, is dramatic; that every composition is an utterance depending on an act of impersonation which it is the duty of the performer or performers to make clear. If, as I believe, Wilson Coker is correct in suggesting that "one can regard the musical work as an organism, a sort of spokesman who addresses listeners,"[6] then the performer, far from being an imperfect intermediary between composer and listener, an inaccurate translator of musical thought, is a living personification of that spokesman—of the mind that experiences the music; or, more clumsily but more precisely, of the mind whose experience the music is.

The most natural approach to a study of such a dramatistic view of musical expression would seem to be through the medium of vocal music, through compositions in which the words may give some clue to the composer's intentions. I therefore propose to begin with some familiar examples of song—which, for the purposes of this discussion, means "art song." That is an unfortunate term, but I know of no other convenient way to designate a lied or a lied-like composition: a song in which a poem (in any language) is set to a precisely composed vocal line united with a fully developed instrumental accompaniment.

I have chosen Schubert's "Erlkönig" not only because the song is so familiar, but also because the poem raises questions that are relevant to this discussion. So let us begin with the poem itself.

> Wer reitet so spät durch Nacht und Wind?
> Es ist der Vater mit seinem Kind;
> Er hat den Knaben wohl in dem Arm,
> Er fasst ihn sicher, er hält ihn warm.

---

[6] Wilson Coker, *Music and Meaning* (New York: The Free Press, 1972), p. 190.

Mein Sohn, was birgst du so bang dein Gesicht?—
Siehst, Vater, du den Erlkönig nicht?
Den Erlenkönig mit Kron' und Schweif?—
Mein Sohn, es ist ein Nebelstreif.—

"Du liebes Kind, komm, geh mit mir!
Gar schöne Spiele spiel' ich mit dir;
Manch bunte Blumen sind an dem Strand,
Meine Mutter hat manch gülden Gewand."

Mein Vater, mein Vater, und hörest du nicht,
Was Erlenkönig mir leise verspricht?—
Sei ruhig, bleibe ruhig, mein Kind;
In dürren Blättern säuselt der Wind.—

"Willst, feiner Knabe, du mit mir gehn?
Meine Töchter sollen dich warten schön;
Meine Töchter führen den nächtlichen Reihn
Und wiegen und tanzen und singen dich ein."

Mein Vater, mein Vater, und siehst du nicht dort
Erlkönigs Töchter am düstern Ort?—
Mein Sohn, mein Sohn, ich seh' es genau,
Es scheinen die alten Weiden so grau.—

"Ich liebe dich, mich reizt deine schöne Gestalt;
Und bist du nicht willig, so brauch' ich Gewalt."
Mein Vater, mein Vater, jetzt fasst er mich an!
Erlkönig hat mir ein Leids getan!—

Dem Vater grauset's, er reitet geschwind,
Er hält in Armen das ächzende Kind,
Erreicht den Hof mit Müh' und Not;
In seinen Armen das Kind war tot.

How is this poem to be read? We know that it was written
as a simulated ballad: an impersonal narrative in simple stanza
form. It is impersonal in the sense that the narrator takes no
part in the story but presents it as an uninvolved and disinterested spectator. The poetic persona refrains from obtruding his

own personality. In some ballads the persona abdicates in favor of the characters in the story: "Lord Randal" and "Edward" are examples of traditional ballads presented entirely as dialogue. In "Erlkönig" there is a dialogue but also, in the first and last stanzas, a narrator. There would appear, then, to be four voices: that of the narrator, who frames the dialogue, and those of the father, the son, and the Erlking. But is this necessarily the case? How do we know that the entire poem is not to be read as only one voice, that of the narrator, who quotes the dialogue of the three characters? Still another possibility is opened by the question and answer in the first stanza. Perhaps this interchange is not a rhetorical device but a real colloquy. In that case the persona would be a double one: the interlocutor and the responder. Here again the responder may be thought of as either framing or quoting the dialogue. The poem may thus be read in at least four ways:

a. One voice: narrator, who quotes the three characters—
N (X, Y, Z);

b. Two voices: interlocutor and responder, who quotes the characters—Q, A (X, Y, Z);

c. Four voices: narrator and characters, who speak for themselves—N, X, Y, Z;

d. Five voices: interlocutor, responder, and characters—
Q, A, X, Y, Z.

One might further question whether the epilogue is necessarily delivered by the narrator of the opening. For example, the question and answer might represent an exchange between two onlookers, the author's persona entering only in the last stanza.

Another set of readings, more subtle than those just enumerated, is suggested by the punctuation. By placing only the Erlking's part in quotation marks and using dashes to set off the words of father and son, Goethe has suggested that the Erlking

7

belongs to another world—perhaps of the son's feverish imagination. I leave it to the reader to work out the various possibilities opened by this conjecture.

What of the song? Schubert, blandly disregarding my elaborate constructions, has adopted the first and simplest reading. (This choice does not require him to make an overt decision as to the reality of the Erlking, but allows him to leave it to the listener's imagination—which may, of course, be influenced by the evocative skill of the singer.) The song is presented by a single narrator who quotes the dialogue. It is clear why this was the most sensible procedure. My analysis, based only on the narrative content of the poem, disregarded the unity of texture imparted by the strict stanza form. The simple regularity of this pattern and the compactness of the whole poem would render a presentation by several actors in dialogue less convincing than a recitation by a single accomplished reader. Similarly, while a literally dramatic performance of the song is possible, it is by no means recommended or even suggested by the score—although Schubert and his friends, on at least one occasion, tried it as a private experiment.[7] It is true that Schubert failed to respect Goethe's stanza form (thereby violating the poet's canons of song composition[8]); nevertheless he imposed his own unity on the vocal line, binding each part to the next in a continuous melodic thread, and he confirmed this unity by the rhythmic ostinato of the accompaniment.

In "Erlkönig" the composer's decision to use a single voice was supported by the form of the poem. Such was by no means

---

[7] See Albert Stadler's account in Otto Erich Deutsch, ed., *Schubert: Memoirs by His Friends*, trans. Rosamond Ley and John Nowell (New York: Macmillan, 1958), p. 153.

[8] See Jack M. Stein, "Was Goethe Wrong about the Nineteenth-Century Lied?" *PMLA*, LXXVII: 3 (June 1962), 232–239. But Goethe apparently relented in his old age. See Edgar Istel, "Goethe and Music," *The Musical Quarterly*, XIV: 2 (April 1928), 216–254, especially p. 221.

the case with "Der Tod und das Mädchen." The Claudius original is frankly dramatic in form:

Das Mädchen:	Vorüber, ach, vorüber,
	Geh, wilder Knochenmann!
	Ich bin noch jung, geh, Lieber;
	Und rühre mich nicht an.
Der Tod:	Gib deine Hand, du schön und zart Gebild!
	Bin Freund und komme nicht zu strafen.
	Sei gutes Muts! ich bin nicht wild,
	Sollst sanft in meinen Armen schlafen!

Furthermore, the two sections of the poem exhibit different verse patterns. Yet here again, Schubert has set his text for a single voice; and although a performance in literal dialogue might be attempted, the musical line is written in such a way as to reward unitary performance. True, the parts assigned to the maiden and Death are distinguishable by range, but Death clearly continues and completes the melodic descent of the maiden. There is also a striking harmonic connection between the two. The maiden's stanza ends with two sequential half-cadences, the first on V of III, the second on the true dominant. Death responds to each of these cadences in turn, for the first of his phrases resolves to III, the second to the tonic (Ex. 1). Here as in "Erlkönig," Schubert's setting invites us to hear the poem not as a dialogue directly presented but as one quoted by a persona; a persona musically represented by a single voice, of basically uniform color, engaged in the protraction of a single melodic line: N (X, Y).

Such personas as those developed by Schubert might be called poetic-vocal personas, or more conveniently, vocal personas, to distinguish them from the purely poetic personas to which they are related but with which they are by no means identical. Obviously they express themselves at least as much by melody as by speech, and as much by tone-color as by phonetic

1. Schubert, "Der Tod und das Mädchen." Note how the line left incomplete by the maiden in m. 19 is taken up and continued, first by the accompaniment, then by Death. The harmonies at mm. 29 and 37 answer and resolve those of mm. 17 and 19.

sound. Another distinction, less obvious but equally significant, applies to all songs with fully realized accompaniment. A poetic persona covers its entire poem: it is the complete voice of the poem. In a play or a dramatic poem, the characters share the poet's voice; but again, what they say covers the entire composition. In contrast, the vocal persona does not cover the entire song; it is not coextensive with the composer's voice, which includes the accompaniment as well. That is why I have called it only the vocal, not the musical persona.

Now, one might try to make an analogy here by maintaining that the accompaniment is a sort of stage direction; and indeed, one sees in "Erlkönig" how the accompaniment can serve as a detailed set of instructions, specifying how fast, how loud, how excitedly, etc., a song should be sung. Perhaps, then, this is the basic function of an accompaniment. Every song is really a little play or monodrama, and we learn what the composer has to tell us by giving exclusive attention to the singers. The same argument would apply a fortiori to opera, where the staging supports the predominance of the actors. But although many opera lovers seem to listen to opera in just this way, most musicians feel that such a response is inadequate. Besides, the analogy fails under the most superficial examination. Stage directions are not meant to be heard, they are at most seen—by those who read the script. Many plays, some of which are by common consent among the greatest ever written, get along very well without their overt use; they are implied in the spoken text. Thus they are not part of the poet's voice: their effect is not direct and verbal, but mediate, through their influence on the actions of the characters and the delivery of their lines. But the accompaniment *is* heard. It is not merely read, it is performed. Its contribution to the total musical structure is indispensable.

In the two cases already examined, for example, the accompaniment reinforces the continuity of the vocal line—in "Erlkönig" by the constant reiteration of basic rhythmic and motivic elements, in "Der Tod und das Mädchen" by anticipating Death's appearance and framing the whole. In fact, these

11

accompaniments would go far toward annulling the disintegrative effects of our hypothetically dramatized renditions—just as accompaniments contribute signally to the unification of the necessarily dramatized presentation of such operatic dialogues as "Là ci darem." And when the accompaniment binds itself as closely to the vocal part as it does at the maiden's words "rühre mich nicht an," first doubling the voice and then continuing the line when the voice is silent (see Ex. 1), it actively contributes to the total discourse of the song. Its personification in the figure of the pianist, or of the orchestral conductor, reminds us that here, too, is a musical consciousness at work. Yet we cannot accept the accompaniment as a character in the drama: not only is it voiceless, communicating only by musical gesture, but obviously it does not inhabit the same world as the vocal persona. Indeed, as we shall see, on one level the singer must pretend to be unaware of the accompanist's existence.

Perhaps a fruitful analogue for the accompanied song might be the narrative. The accompaniment would then correspond to the part of the narrator—not one who is a participating character in his own story, but one who, like the storyteller in reading *a* of "Erlkönig," describes events in which he does not take part. The relationship can be made clear in the form of a mathematical proportion:

Accompaniment: Vocal persona:: Narrator: Poetic character

The comparison is tempting and in some respects illuminating, for, like a narrator, the accompaniment often seems to evoke and to comment on the words and the implied actions of the persona portrayed by the singer. From this point of view the accompaniment would be considered as the most direct representative of the composer's voice—or, as I should like to put it, of the complete musical persona. The vocal persona, on the other hand, is now reduced in status to the embodiment of a character quoted by the complete persona (like the father or the son in our first "Erlkönig" model).

Odd as it may seem to think of a song in this way, our new analogy offers the advantage of presenting voice and accompaniment together as a unified utterance of the composer's voice. At the same time it distinguishes between the two media of expression in such a way as to make it theatrically appropriate for them to be represented in performance by the two figures of singer and instrumentalist. Furthermore, it provides a justification—if one is needed—for Schubert's transformation of the dramatic dialogue of "Der Tod und das Mädchen" into an implied narrative. The entire song can be interpreted from the single point of view of the accompaniment: "Death is approaching. The agitated maiden says . . . Death replies calmly . . . Death enfolds her in his arms."

But what about opera? If all song is narrative, then an opera must be a narrative as well—a novel and not a play. The complete musical persona is telling us about the characters, and their parts should be thought of as if within quotation marks. On the stage the singer does not portray a dramatic character directly but represents a character in a narrative. He is enacting the musical persona's conception of the character; that is, he is quoting rather than talking. Strange as this view may seem, there is something to be said for it. In music drama of the Wagnerian type it is certainly true that the over-arching control of the composite musical line, working through orchestra and voice alike, implies the primacy of a single point of view to an extent that would be inconceivable in a spoken play. But even in the more traditional operas, based on discrete musical forms interspersed with recitative or spoken dialogue, successive and simultaneous musical lines, both vocal and instrumental, are shaped into a unity that cannot be the work of any one character or even of any group of characters on the stage; this unity forces us to look for a wider intelligence at work and hence to assume the constant presence of a single musical persona.

Only if the instrumental element were reduced to the point of negligibility and if the songs were not only discrete but so widely dispersed that they could not be heard as part of an overall sequence could the work be heard as free from this persona's hegemony. But then it would scarcely be an opera, but rather a play with music. Is it not, after all, our constant sense of the presence of a musical persona, even during the dialogue, that makes of *Die Zauberflöte* a full-fledged opera and not a mere *Singspiel?* Herein lies its great superiority over *Die Entführung aus dem Serail*, delightful though that work is. When Sarastro speaks we accept Mozart's decision that he should not sing, but when the Pasha speaks we feel that Mozart has failed to provide him with music. When spoken dialogue is successful, the absence of music can be felt as part of the design. One should always feel grateful when the music returns, but one should never find oneself disappointed by the composer's failure to provide it (as in the case of the Pasha) or distracted by the extension of nonmusical episodes (such as the jailer's scene in *Die Fledermaus*).

This way of looking at song also explains why melodrama usually proves to be an unsatisfactory mixture on the concert stage but can work when judiciously applied to an appropriate operatic scene. On the concert stage the poetic persona has been insufficiently, if at all, subjected to musical control. Since it has not been transformed into a vocal persona, it cannot be accepted as part of the composer's voice, with which it must try to establish an uneasy partnership. Even the adoption of *Sprechstimme* may not completely solve the problem, although Schoenberg evidently felt that it went far enough in the direction of song to establish a true vocal persona. In opera, on the other hand, the spoken part, like pure dialogue, becomes a segment of the complete vocal characterization that has established itself in song. We can thus accept the melodrama in *Fidelio* as a passage in which the composer, for purposes of mood and atmosphere, has temporarily assigned to his characters the tone-color and rhythms of actual speech against the commentary of a musical accompaniment.

The analogy between accompaniment and narrator, then, appears to be helpful; but can it be sustained? Is it not contrary to all experience to maintain that the singing voice embodies a personality somehow less complete than the character presented by the speaking voice in a normal play, or even than that shadowy figure, the musical persona, which we are supposed to infer from the presence of instrumental accompaniment and its interaction with the voice? Common sense tells us that something is wrong. If the singing voice and the accompaniment inhabit different worlds, then the world of the voice is the one we accept as closer to our own. Any analogy constructed to clarify the relation of voice to accompaniment must take into account this elementary reaction.

Actually there is no model that will do justice to the complexity of the simplest accompanied song—except that of song itself. One art can never be explained in terms of another. But there is one model that retains the helpful features of the rejected analogue and at the same time suggests a more acceptable relationship between the vocal and instrumental components. Let us look again at one of the possible ways of reading "Erlkönig," the one I have labelled c. This reading conveys a mixed form, both narrative (for the beginning and ending) and dramatic (for the dialogue). Such a reading implies both a narrative persona and dramatic characters. And although this may not be the best way to read the *poem*, it suggests an illuminating approach to the *song*—or to any song. On this view, the accompaniment is still the analogue of a narrative voice, and our formula still holds:

Accompaniment: Vocal persona:: Narrator: Poetic character

Now, however, in accordance with reading *c*, the vocal line of the song and the words of the characters in the poem are to be construed, not as quoted by the narrator, but as presented directly. Thus the vocal persona has become a full dramatic character in its own right—or, in the case of opera, a complete cast of characters.

Literary mixed forms of this kind are not uncommon. The traditional musical settings of the Passions treat the biblical text as just this kind of drama, with the Evangelist and the characters of his narrative sharing the stage. Clearly such a reading was not the author's intention here, but in other cases a similar mixture is inherent in the literary form. Think of Cocteau's libretto for Stravinsky's *Oedipus*, which presents its narrator and its mythical characters as equally real (although inhabiting different regions of reality, as symbolized by the contrast between the vernacular of the narrator and the Latin of the characters). Think of *Bleak House*, which alternates sections told by the author's own persona with others supposedly written by one of the characters, Esther Summerson. In both cases the author speaks in two different guises, or sets of guises: as a narrative persona, and as one or more of the characters. But these characters are not merely quoted: they are given equal standing with the narrative persona and are allowed to speak for themselves.

According to our revised model, the situation in song and opera is similar. The composer speaks with double voice, through a musical persona that assumes a double guise. The message of the accompaniment is direct, for it is not mediated by the words of a specific personality but is communicated through the gestures of the music alone; yet for this reason it seems veiled by comparison with the message of the voice. In the vocal line the persona speaks only through a dramatic character that expresses itself in words as well as in musical gestures, but as a result this line enjoys an explicitness that the mute instrumental part lacks.

The art of song thus exploits a dual form of utterance, related to but not to be confused with the dual medium of voice and instrument. It combines the explicit language of words with a medium that depends on the movements implied by nonverbal sounds and therefore might best be described as a continuum of symbolic gesture. In this respect, then, song differs from its literary model, which of course employs a consistently verbal medium. Nor can the narrative and dramatic components of the literary form hope to enjoy the simultaneity of voice and accompaniment that is normal in music. These discrepancies, and others that will arise as we proceed, may cast doubt on the validity of our analogy; nevertheless, it remains useful for the time being at least. The analogy permits the arguments based on the preceding model without opposing the judgments of common sense. It insists that the composer's voice is to be heard, not in the vocal line alone, but in a progression that synthesizes voice with accompaniment, and explicit with symbolic utterance. At the same time it explains and justifies the personal superiority that always seems proper to the vocal part, even when that part is not in complete charge. Finally, singers portray characters, just as legitimate actors do; yet the concept of the quasi-narrative accompaniment establishes the accompanist (or the conductor) as a dramatically appropriate figure.

There is thus a triad of personas, or persona-like figures, involved in the accompanied song: the vocal, the instrumental, and the (complete) musical. Without pursuing the analogy too far, one can note certain correspondences between this trinity and that of Christian dogma. The song as a whole is the utterance—the creation—of the complete musical persona. Like the Father, this persona "begets" in the vocal persona a Son that embodies its Word; and it produces in the accompaniment a "Holy Spirit" that speaks to us directly, without the mediation of the Word.[9]

Of the three, only the vocal persona—again like the Son— can be thought of as "incarnate," since it is the only one that expresses itself fully through the human voice. By comparison with its forthright existence, the instrumental persona may seem a creature of analogy, an imaginary construct. Let us therefore call it a *virtual persona,* invoking a concept that will be analyzed in detail during the discussion of purely instrumental music.

The complete musical persona is to be inferred from the interaction of the other two, so let us call it an *implicit persona.* Although its medium is a compound arising from a mixture of the vocal and the instrumental, it is held together by the unifying power of the musical line. As the vehicle of the composer's complete message, it can also be called *the composer's persona.* Note, however, that this means not "*the* persona of the composer" but "*a* persona of the composer"; for the persona of each composition is uniquely created by and for that composition. And because in song the complete musical persona embraces both vocal and instrumental components, the composer's persona governs words as well as music. The words, that is, have become a part of the composer's message, utterances of his own voice. In a sense, he composes his own text.

[9] It is an interesting and perhaps instructive exercise to compare various musical styles on the basis of the extent to which the *filioque* phrase can be applied to the procession of the Holy Spirit of each.

Some poems are designed to be set to music, others are written with no such intent. No matter: in either case the song composer considers that the poem is his to use. For a song is not primarily the melodic recitation or the musical interpretation or the criticism of a poem. Although it may be any or all of these it is first of all a new creation of which the poem is only one component. The familiar pun that accuses composers of using texts as pretexts goes too far, but it contains an element of truth nevertheless. The composer is not primarily engaged in "setting" a poem. As I have pointed out elsewhere, a composer cannot "set" a poem directly, for in this sense there is no such thing as "the poem": what he uses is one reading of the poem—that is to say, a specific performance, for even a silent reading is a kind of performance.[10] He must consider all aspects of the poem that are not realizable in this performance as irrelevant. And to say that he "sets" even this reading is less accurate than to say that he appropriates it: he makes it his own by turning it into music. What we hear in a song, then, is not the poet's persona but the composer's.

A passage from Eliot's essay comes to mind here. Discussing the difference between a dramatic monologue and a play, he insists that "what we normally hear . . . in the dramatic monologue is the voice of the poet. . . . In *The Tempest*, it is Caliban who speaks; in 'Caliban upon Setebos' it is Browning's voice that we hear, Browning talking aloud through Caliban."[11] Whether or not Eliot is right about the dramatic monologue, what he says illuminates the distinction between poem and song. The parallel should be clear. In the poem, it is the poet who speaks, albeit in the voice of a persona. In the song, it is the composer who speaks, in part through the words of the poet.

[10] See my article "Words into Music," in Northrop Frye, ed., *Sound and Poetry*, English Institute Essays 1956, (New York: Columbia University Press, 1957), pp. 3–15.
[11] *Op. cit.*, p. 13.

2

Persona, Protagonist, and Characters

The concept of song as an utterance of the composer's voice may be clarified by contrast with an opposing view, that of Goethe himself. He praised Zelter for producing "compositions [that] I feel to be, so to speak, identical with my songs."[1] Zelter, for his part, felt that he was merely embodying the poet's own musical intuitions: "I respect the form of the poem and try to recognize my poet therein, for I imagine him as having a melody of his own hovering in mind, insofar as he is a poet in this sense of the word too. If I can enter into rapport with him, and strike off his melody so accurately that he himself feels at home with it, then our melody will prove enjoyable as well."[2] Both conceived of song as a medium in which the poet speaks through the composer. The composer's job is consequently either to find the unique music implied by the only possible reading of the poem, or else to devise music so neutral that it would fit any reading. Zelter was trying to achieve the former, but most of us today would agree that he only succeeded in accomplishing the latter.

Neither Goethe nor Zelter understood what Schubert instinctively realized. I have suggested that, to a composer like Schubert, a poem is only raw material. What he deals with is not the poem but his reading of it. He appropriates that reading and makes it a component in another work, entirely his own—a

---

[1] Max Hecker, ed., *Der Briefwechsel zwischen Goethe und Zelter* (Leipzig: Insel-Verlag, 1913), Vol. II, p. 59.
[2] Ibid., Vol. II, pp. 262–263.

larger form created by the musical setting. The poem can no longer be heard as independent, for it is modified by a vocal line requiring in its own turn further completion by an accompaniment that prepares it, explains it, and places it in a larger context. The process involves a modification, often a thorough-going mutation, of such phonetic elements as accent and vowel quality; what is more interesting in the present context is the inevitable transformation of poetic and dramatic content. Specifically, the poetic persona is transformed into what we have hitherto called the vocal persona: a character in a kind of mono-dramatic opera, who sings the original poem as his part. To emphasize this role, I shall henceforth refer to such a vocal persona as the *protagonist* of a song.

If every song is to a certain extent a little opera, every opera is no less an expanded song. Opera, although it appears superficially to be a purely dramatic form, is as much a mixture of the narrative and the dramatic as individual song. For here too one can clearly distinguish the trinity of vocal, instrumental, and complete musical personas; here too the composer's persona comments directly, through the orchestra, on that portion of its message that is mediated through the characters.

In both song and opera the music transforms the personalities projected by the original poetic text in two apparently contradictory ways: it simultaneously particularizes them and universalizes them. By specifying the tempi, the dynamics, the exact rhythms, and the pitch inflections that are to be applied to the words, the music bestows upon each character a peculiarly vivid individuality. At the same time, this character participates in, and is largely formed by, an all-encompassing environment of nonverbal sound—an environment to which he in turn contributes through his own melodic line and vocal timbre. And because we as audience are bathed in the same sound, we can feel this environment as ours. To the extent that we do so, we tend to interpret the vocal character in terms of our own sympathies and emotions, and to feel ourselves involved in his. Each of us can thus participate in the sonic environment and hence, to a certain extent, in the nature of the character who comes to life by virtue of that environment. This is what I mean by saying that the poetic persona or character is universalized: the vocal character implicates in his own world every sympathetic member of the world of his audience, and every such listener shares the character's experience.

This reaction can occur only if the listener can in some way accept the character's reality. But how can this be? The well-composed song should convince the listener that the composer's voice is both musical and verbal—that the implicit musical persona, surrounding and including the protagonist, is creating words, vocal line, and accompaniment simultaneously. How, then, within this verbal-musical complex, can the protagonist appear to live out his own role—to compose his own part as it were?

The problem here is closely related to that of theatrical illusion in general. There could be no drama if we did not accept what we know in fact to be false: that the actors *are* the characters, who are living their parts and making up their lines as they go along. More than that: the principle that some form of dramatic impersonation underlies all literature means that all modes of imaginative writing are united in implying a basic simulation. The lyric pretends that its persona is composing the poem; the novel pretends that its narrator is telling the story. The reader must go along with the pretense, else he cannot derive emotional satisfaction from the poem or enjoy the suspense of the story.

If we take the art of song seriously, we must accord the same faith to the characters portrayed by singers. They are not mere puppets, controlled by the composer's strings. They are more like Petrouchkas, brought to life by the composer, but thenceforth driven by their own wills and desires. Thus the vocal persona adopts the original simulation of the poetic persona and adds another of his own: he "composes," not the words alone, but the vocal line as well. We admittedly connive at this pretense when we watch an opera, but we should realize that a similar situation must obtain if we really attend to a performance of a Schubert lied. For if we try to follow words as well as music, we must accept the song, no less than the opera, as a dramatic presentation.

Some conventions of performance afford evidence that we do intuitively think of songs in this way. On the modern dramatic stage in Western countries, women may occasionally take men's roles—especially young men's; but the reverse is rare and is probably acceptable only for humorous or grotesque effects. What is interesting is that we have transferred these theatrical conventions to the concert stage, where we apply them to nonoperatic song. Thus we accept the performance of *Dichterliebe* by a woman, but not of *Frauenliebe* by a man—although we would permit a man to sing a narrative in which a woman's voice is quoted. The singer is the actual, living embodiment of the vocal protagonist—he is the persona turned into a person; and we insist on a modicum of congruence within the framework of our usual stage conventions.

Probably the singer's first task is to determine the nature of the protagonist—to ask, "Who am I?" The answer is never simple. Just as we conceive of the composer's own persona as operating in three areas—verbal, vocal, and instrumental—so we interpret the protagonist as moving on three levels simultaneously: the poetic, which is strictly verbal; the vocal, which conjoins the words with a melodic line; and the vocal-instrumental, which embeds the line in the total musical texture.

The character that results may have little in common with his purely poetic original. We have already seen how Schubert reduced the two speakers of "Der Tod und das Mädchen" to quotations by a single impersonator. Much more subtle is the transformation he has worked on the narrator of "Erlkönig." Goethe, imitating the traditional ballad style, tells the story in a detached manner that contrasts ironically with the emotions implied by the quoted dialogue. Schubert's narrator is anything but detached. The dominant of his opening question has to wait for twelve measures before it receives its tonic answer, and these measures include a modulation, through the subdominant, to the relative major—a progression that, by predicting the main course of events in the first stanzas of dialogue, involves the narrator inextricably in the fate of his characters (Ex. 2). The accompaniment reinforces this effect by its insistence on the stormy setting and the galloping hooves. And as

these sounds die away at the end of the ride, leaving the recitative with its oddly broken conclusion, we feel that the narrator is participating in the father's shocked discovery—either that he is actually present at the scene or that he has recreated it so vividly that his imagination has conjured it up before him.

Our analysis of song as an analogue of a mixed narrative-dramatic model thus implies that every song (or opera) can be heard in two ways: as the experience on the one hand of the

2. Schubert, "Erlkönig." The dominant of m. 19, marking the end of the narrator's question, reaches a definitive tonic only in m. 32, after excursions to IV and III. These progressions foreshadow important key areas to be established later at mm. 40, 54–58, and 85.

composer's persona (the implicit musical persona), and on the other of the vocal protagonist (or characters). The resulting tension between the motivations of the composer's persona (toward "form") and those of the character (toward "freedom of personal expression") is especially noticeable in opera, where the theatrical illusion helps to establish and maintain the concrete individuality of the characters.

Among opera composers, Mozart was notably successful in creating characters who appear to move independently and voluntarily, yet who fit easily and naturally into the design of the whole. In his operas each of the three levels, verbal, vocal, and vocal-instrumental, complements the others so effectively that one can accept the unitary result as representing equally the thought of the complete musical persona and the wills of his characters. Look, for example, at the opening section of "Dove sono" (Ex. 3). First read the bare text, which outlines

3. Mozart, *The Marriage of Figaro*, "Dove sono." The connecting beams indicate linear relationships between the voice and the accompaniment. Thus in mm. 1–5 the strings double the melody and the woodwinds provide transitions between its phrase members. In mm. 5–8 the string doubling descends into an inner voice, but in m. 7 the first violin again begins to echo the voice's downward motion, although at a faster rate. An even more extreme diminution of the same line is provided by the oboe in mm. 8–9. The second large phrase is similarly treated; but note the added complexity of the intermingled string and vocal lines at the climax in mm. 15–16.

the Countess's view of her situation. Add to this the vocal line, and the intensity of her reaction is vividly projected. Now fit this to its accompaniment, and observe how the instrumental line clarifies, amplifies, and completes the voice part, placing it in the context, not of this song alone but, by virtue of the orchestral sound, of the entire opera.

When Wagner further integrated the musical context by extending the orchestral sound throughout each act and by using repetitive motifs, he effected a subtle but profound change of emphasis. In the number opera the separation of each aria or ensemble draws attention to the specific character or characters involved. In a work of the Wagnerian type, as I have already pointed out, the continuity of the orchestral sound and of the musical design constantly refers to an all-inclusive persona surveying the entire action from a single point of view.

Roughly, one could say that whereas the control of Mozart's persona never inhibits the individuality of his characters, the vitality of Wagner's characters never threatens the dominance of his persona. The two composers thus offer contrasting solutions to a basic problem: how to reconcile the formal requirements of the musico-dramatic composition with the lifelike tendencies of the characters. The tension between the demands of design and of representation is one that the arts of song and opera share with many others, and it is a source of artistic vitality.[3]

The vocal persona—whether protagonist of a song or character in an opera—is subject to another tension as well, one that is peculiar to his medium. Let me approach this point by asking

---

[3] See my "Music: a View from Delft," *The Musical Quarterly*, XLVII: 4 (Oct. 1961), 439–453, reprinted in Benjamin Boretz and Edward T. Cone, eds., *Perspectives on Contemporary Music Theory* (New York: W. W. Norton, 1972), pp. 57–71.

an odd question: does a vocal persona know he is singing? Of course the *singer* knows he is singing, but what about the character the singer portrays? The dramatic circumstances in most cases make it highly inappropriate that he should be aware of singing: he is telling a story, or measuring a floor, or making love, or expressing his anger, or praying, or dying. From the point of view of the implied or enacted drama, he is not "really" singing at all. It follows that he must be unaware of the accompaniment as well. Again, note the distinction between singer and character: of course the *singer* must be aware of the accompaniment. But although we know that he gets his pitch, meter, and tempo from the accompaniment—and often his thematic material as well—it would destroy the illusion were he to indicate this overtly by gesture or facial expression. Lucia must synchronize perfectly with her flute, but she must not reveal that she is conscious of its presence. (Once in a while this rule may be deliberately broken for humorous effect. Figaro can get a laugh by reacting in exaggerated fashion to the mocking horns at the end of "Aprite un po'.")

Even when the accompaniment produces programmatically appropriate sounds, it is rarely to be considered as directly heard by the vocal persona. The protagonist of "Der Leiermann" hears a hurdy-gurdy, but he does not hear what the actual singer and the audience hear: a pianist playing a stylized version of what a hurdy-gurdy might sound like. Even less realistic are the horses's hooves in the background of "Erlkönig," which formalize those presumably imagined by the storyteller. In both cases the sound as heard or imagined by the protagonist is only raw material; what the singer and his audience hear is the composer's transformation of the sound into an element of the accompaniment.

The importance of these distinctions becomes clear if we contrast the normal state of an operatic character with his behavior in situations where the libretto requires him to *enact* the singing of a song. Cherubino, for example, realizes that he is singing "Voi che sapete," for it is a canzonetta that he has composed and is performing for the Countess. Similarly, he must hear Suzanna accompany him, and he must let the audience know that he hears her. Moreover, for the duration of the song, he impersonates the protagonist of that song. He plays a role within a role, shifting the simulation of "unawareness" to another level.

(It is not always true, however, that a character "singing" in this fashion is aware of his accompaniment. When Verdi's Desdemona "sings" her "Salce," and Berlioz's Marguerite her "Roi de Thule," both are obviously conscious of "singing," but neither can "hear" her accompaniment, for in each case the accompaniment is purely orchestral and not dramatically accounted for as in the Mozart example. One might also question whether such a character can always be thought of as realistically "singing" what we hear. In the case of Marguerite, for example, it could be argued that the composer has substituted, for the folklike tune appropriate to her simplicity and presumably restricted musical ability, a highly sophisticated melody more expressive of her inner emotional state.)

From a realistic point of view, then, it appears that we must usually assume the singing character to be unconscious of his musical environment. Yet this interpretation, unmodified, fails to do justice to the complexity of the act of song, and to the subtlety of the transformation of the poetic into the vocal persona. It requires us to accept a vocal character's projection of a coherent melodic line, together with its harmonization with the accompaniment and its musical relationships with other vocal lines, as adventitious—as proceeding in no way from the personality and motivations of the character himself. To be sure, one could argue that all these musical values are purely

decorative accessories, contributing formal elegance to an artificial dramatic construct and at the same time affording the
audience added sensuous delight. This theory may well apply
to some styles of song writing and to some genres of theater
music, and it may please some strictly formalist estheticians,
but it is insufficient to satisfy those who insist that music can
produce a powerfully expressive effect through a dramatically
apposite relationship to its text.

Perhaps, then, the music should be considered as a mode
of representation through which a character is realized (as a
portrait is realized through lines and colors), which controls
our perception of the character (as a style of brushwork affects
our view of the subject), yet which is fundamentally external
to the character (as a portrait is to be distinguished from the
person portrayed). According to this theory, the music, proceeding entirely and directly from the consciousness of the
composer's persona, could be dramatically appropriate and
highly expressive, yet outside the represented world of the character, and hence totally unperceived by him. Now, I do not wish
to discuss whether any represented object can ever be considered as independent of its mode of representation. I suspect
that it cannot—that the personality apparently recorded in a
portrait is actually a personality specifically created by the portrait. But even if one maintained the independence of object
and mode of representation in painting, it would be hard to
apply the analogy to song. For here part of the means of representation—singing—is assigned to the character himself. It is
not merely a means by which we view the character; it is part
of the way he expresses himself. The act of singing is hard to
imagine as anything other than voluntary, and hence we can
scarcely consider it as basically external to the character—as,
say, representing a direct comment of the implicit persona

rather than symbolizing an intentional gesture on the part of the character.

Accordingly, every singing persona seems to be subject to a tension between the verbal and the vocal aspects of his personality. From the realistic verbal point of view, such a character is unaware of singing, and of being accompanied. Yet on the musical levels he must in some sense be aware of both. How are these two aspects to be reconciled?

A solution becomes possible if we conceive the contrast between the verbal and the vocal as a symbolic parallel to the contrast between the conscious and subconscious components of the personality. "Subconscious," as I use it, is not intended to convey any psychoanalytic connotations. Perhaps "subliminal" would be a better term, but that too now carries with it specific, and unfortunate, suggestions. By "the subconscious" I mean a realm of psychic experience that extends all the way from the deep repressions of the Freudian unconscious to a level just below that of fully conscious, fully articulated thought. It is a realm of attitudes, feelings, impulses, and motivations, unverbalized either because they are essentially unverbalizable, or because they have not risen to the level of explicit articulation in the mind of the subject.

The way in which the distinction between the conscious and the subconscious, as so defined, applies to song can be made clear by a reference to some everyday experiences we all have. "Don't raise your voice."—"I wasn't raising my voice."— "Yes, you were."—"I'm sorry, I didn't mean to." Or: "Don't talk so fast."—"I didn't realize I was." When we speak, we are normally completely conscious of the words we use, but much less so of our inflections of tone, pitch, loudness, rhythm, and speed. Often when we are excited or deeply moved we are entirely unaware of them. Singing, in its nonverbal aspects, emphasizes just these components of speech and subjects them to artistic control. Its power derives from its articulation and intensification of these usually amorphous elements. "I understand a fury in your words,/ But not the words," says Desdemona: it is this fury that would come to full expression in song (and has notably done so in Verdi's music: not Otello's conscious anger, but the rage beneath the surface, which takes control of him and drives him to his doom).

Actually there is a subconscious element in the verbal component as well. Speech is language projected by voice. Just as singing intensifies the expressive power of the sound of the voice through the formalization of its inflections, poetry—like good prose, for that matter—intensifies the expressive powers of the language through the formalization of the choice and ordering of words. Here too, as in song, such formalization must take place outside the conscious thought of the characters: we cannot suppose that Hamlet realizes he is speaking English blank verse instead of Danish prose. Hamlet's use of English is a necessary convention, without which Shakespeare would have been unable to write the play, or many of us to understand it; but the elevated verse he employs is an expressive medium that permits the voicing of emotions and thoughts usually unverbalized at the conscious level of ordinary speech. Nevertheless, the "level of subconsciousness" presented by an art that deals with words must lie nearer the surface than the one presented by an art of pure sound. This is what Roger Sessions is getting at when he says: " 'Emotion' is specific, individual and conscious; music goes deeper than this, to the energies which animate our psychic life. . . . It reproduces for us the most intimate essence, the tempo and the energy, of our spiritual being . . . —all, in fact, of the fine shades of dynamic variation of our inner life. It reproduces these far more directly and more specifically than is possible through any other medium of human communication."[4] So when, as in song, a musical line is combined with a text, it is natural for us to accept the music as referring to a subconscious level underlying—and lying under—whatever thoughts and emotions are expressed by the words.

The accompaniment, it will be remembered, is the direct component of the implicit persona. At the same time, its subject matter must be closely related to that of the vocal line. That is to say, in dramatistic terms, the instrumental persona conveys certain aspects of the subconscious of the vocal protagonist, but indirectly. It thus neatly complements the vocal line, which is the direct expression of the protagonist but the indirect component of the implicit persona. But the accompaniment may also refer to the environment of the character (as in "Erlkönig" or "Der Leiermann"), or to his actions, gestures, and physical condition. It is thus evidently "conscious" of the character—as a narrative persona must be. It can present either the character's point of view or its own, or a combination of the two. That is how accompanied ensembles are possible, for the instrumental persona, like an omniscient author, understands the motivations of all the participants. That, also, is how the orchestra can reveal who Siegmund's father really was, and can prophesy the occasion on which Siegfried will experience fear. Finally, that is why an accompanist, who symbolizes the virtual persona, may openly acknowledge the presence of the singer who must simulate unawareness of him.

The accompaniment does something else as well. By placing the voice in a larger formal context—a more connected melodic line, a clearer harmonic progression, a more complete rhythmic design—it symbolically suggests both the impingement of the outer world on the individual represented by the vocal persona, and the subconscious reaction of the individual

[4] "The Composer and His Message," in Augusto Centeno, ed., *The Intent of the Artist* (Princeton: Princeton University Press, 1941), pp. 123–124.

to this impingement. That is why, in "Erlkönig" and "Der Leiermann" we hear, not the actual sounds of hooves and hurdy-gurdy, but a transformation of those sounds—their resonance in the subconscious of the protagonist as interpreted by the consciousness of the instrumental persona. Thus, even when the accompaniment appears to be dealing with external circumstances, it is usually revealing their effect on the protagonist. It is appropriate, then, that he should let the accompaniment prophesy his key, his tempo, even his melodic material: he is "composing" his part in response to the circumstances thus symbolized, just as his words are a response to an implicit or explicit dramatic situation. So it is wrong to imagine him as completely "unconscious" of the accompaniment. True, he is not *aware* of it; that is, he does not realize that he is "hearing" it. But we might say that although he is not conscious of it he is "subconscious" of it. Consciously, he neither knows that he is singing nor hears the accompaniment; but his subconscious both knows and hears.

On the other hand, there are many occasions when the fact that a character subconsciously "hears" the accompaniment need not imply that he understands all its dramatic implications. Indeed, there are times when he obviously does not know everything that the instrumental persona knows. Siegmund certainly does not understand the significance of the Walhalla motif by which the orchestra identifies for us his vanished father, nor does Siegfried comprehend the prophecy of the magic fire by which the orchestra foretells the occasion of his first and only fear. In this regard, Wagner's orchestra has sometimes been compared to a "collective unconscious," in which each character participates according to his own knowledge and ability. To a certain extent every accompaniment is like this. Whether it is taken as symbolizing the individual or the collective unconscious, or Nature, or the Voice of God—or none of these—it must be assumed to be available to every character in question; but what the character makes of it depends on his own potentialities.

At this point it should be clear that the mixed narrative-dramatic form is no longer a valid literary model for song. We do not normally think of literary characters as "hearing" the narrative that presents them. We might try to retain the analogy by insisting that the vocal character's subconscious perception of the accompaniment is to be interpreted symbolically: as a relationship, not with the actual accompaniment (narrative) but with the environment symbolized by the accompaniment (the events that the narrative expounds); yet this would submit the comparison to severe strain for no good reason. Our model has done its work; let us dismiss it. In the last analysis, there is only one literary analogue rich enough and complex enough to come near serving as a model for accompanied song or for opera, and in adducing it I promise that it will be the last one. It is the mixed form par excellence: the nameless genre of *Ulysses*. Here Joyce's protean persona moves in and out of the thoughts of his characters; here narrative, dramatic, and esoteric techniques are combined; here conscious and subconscious persistently interpenetrate each other. Joyce was, as we know, a trained musician, and his novel is an opera in words.

The usefulness of the foregoing analysis can be tested by applying it to some problematical examples. "Mir ist so wunderbar" is one. What is the dramatic relevance of the canon? Beautiful though it is, it attaches identical music to diverse words sung by a motley quartet. But this is no ordinary ensemble. It is not a conversation but a fourfold soliloquy in which each character comments on a situation that three of them misinterpret. Only Leonora knows the truth, and she must conceal it. Thus the conscious thoughts of the characters—their words—are various. Yet the canonic device implies, through the identity of the melodic lines, that the intuitions of the deceived ones have somehow led them to a subconscious appreciation of the real state of affairs—perhaps not of the truth about Leonora's disguise, but at least of the truth about her character. Each of them, even Jaquino, is touched by her nobility, as the canon makes clear. The accompaniment, expressing the instrumental persona's synoptic understanding of the complex relationships, reinforces the unity of the group and emphasizes the significance of this moment of truth by enveloping the vocal polyphony with the mysteriously hushed sound of a unique orchestral texture.

The quartet performs an important musico-dramaturgical function. An audience watching *Fidelio* is, ideally speaking, as much in the dark about the nature of the leading character as her companions are. So far, the libretto has given no hint of Fidelio's identity. And though even the most ignorant opera goer will presumably have read a synopsis, or at least glanced at the tell-tale cast of characters, it is nevertheless artistically necessary to suggest at this point, by musico-dramatic means, the basic motivation of the plot. Through "Mir ist so wunderbar" the relatively omniscient musical persona prepares the audience for the full revelation that is soon to come.

It is interesting to contrast Beethoven's canon with that of Mozart in *Così fan tutte*. As has often been pointed out, Guglielmo's inability to carry his imitative part in "È nel tuo, nel mio bicchiero" reflects his rage, which makes it impossible for him to mask his true feelings by accepting the words and music of the canon. What is not often asked is whether Ferrando, by joining in with the two ladies (musically as well as verbally), expresses his acquiescence in a situation that he has hitherto deplored—or perhaps has only seemed to. One has the suspicion that Ferrando has enjoyed the whole charade and might not be averse to the change of fiancées! Is this really the case?

The answer is not easy. It depends on how successfully music can seem to mask as well as explore a character's true attitudes—and on how one can tell which it is doing. In depicting a character consciously playing a deceptive role, the composer may choose to emphasize either his real subconscious nature or that of his assumed role. Mozart's solution to the problem throughout *Così fan tutte* is typically subtle and ambiguous. By contrast, it is almost always easy to determine which method Verdi has chosen in his treatment of Iago, which shows clear examples of each. Compare the devious chromatics in Iago's narration of Cassio's dream with the straightforward diatonicism of the oath duet: in the first instance his basic untrustworthiness is symbolized by the side-slipping harmonic progressions; in the second, he appears to be as honest as Otello himself. Here the deceit penetrates to a much deeper level, for with magnificent cynicism Iago's subconscious apes Otello's own.

Schubert's settings of Heine's texts in *Schwanengesang* have sometimes been criticized for their failure to appreciate the poet's fundamentally ironic approach.[5] To be sure, Schubert's protagonist is not Heine's—nor, if I am right, should one expect him to be. The texts of the songs, we must remember, are now Schubert's. Even so, we may still regret the composer's apparent insensitivity to the poet's mordancy. One glaring case is "Am Meer," which seems to miss completely the bitterness of the concluding reference to the poisonous tears:

> Mich hat das unglückselge Weib
> Vergiftet mit ihren Tränen.

[5] See Jack M. Stein, *Poem and Music in the German Lied from Gluck to Hugo Wolf* (Cambridge: Harvard University Press, 1971), pp. 80–91.

But it may be that Schubert adds yet one more irony to Heine's. Perhaps the sentimental ending of the song, returning as it does to the moment when the girl's tears fell "liebevoll," is the composer's way of indicating that, whatever the poetic persona may feel, the vocal protagonist is subconsciously still in love with the "unglückselge Weib." In the same way, at the end of "Der Doppelgänger," the moving setting of the words "So manche Nacht, in alter Zeit" insists that the hero, beneath his self-mockery, unconsciously realizes that the emotions he is trying to disparage are valid and still very much alive. Indeed, a subtle motivic connection suggests that a common theme— of emotional truth?—underlies the nightmare vision of this song, the posturing of "Der Atlas," the apparent levity of "Das Fischermädchen," and the self-pity of "Ihr Bild" (Ex. 4). Was

4. Schubert, songs from *Schwanengesang*.

Schubert aware of this double layer of irony, which can be read into all his Heine songs? Whether he was or not, they are the richer for being heard in this way.

3

On Birthdays and Other
Occasions for Song

The discussion so far has been restricted to one narrowly defined type of song. This word has designated both a single method of composition and a single mode of performance. It has been assumed that the composer begins with a previously existing text, which he adapts as the verbal component of a musical work designed to be sung by a soloist (or, in the case of an operatic ensemble, a group of soloists) with instrumental accompaniment. But we know that there are other ways of writing songs and of performing them. To what extent are the concepts developed in the foregoing arguments applicable to the wider range of vocal literature?

Take, for example, the contention that the composer appropriates his own reading of a preexisting poem in order to use it as one component of a new work of art, and that what we then hear in the words is less the poet speaking than the composer through the poet. Suppose, however, that the composer has set his own words. How does the analysis apply now?

We must distinguish between two types of poet-composer. The first uses words that he has previously written with no express intention of setting them to music. His creative role as composer is then entirely separate from his role as poet. It is mere coincidence, so to speak, that composer and poet happen to be the same man. He may have written the poem twenty years before, or the day before—no matter. The composer appropriates the text for purposes beyond those for which it was designed. He fastens upon it a single reading—granted, a reading that may claim greater authenticity than one by a composer less familiar with the poem, yet a reading that equally delimits its meaning. When this reading is set to music, the effective voice is no longer the poet's but the composer's.

The second type is the poet-composer who, like Campion or like Wagner, uses words that he has written for just that purpose. Now the resultant voice is even more strongly that of the poet-composer as composer, for as poet he never intended his text to stand independently. He designed it for appropriation, and he probably wrote it with the specific reading in mind that he knew he would later utilize as composer. As a result the poem suffers less from its inevitable transformation than a self-sufficient text does. The gap between the original poem and the composer's reading is minimal, and for this reason some may feel that songs of this kind are the most satisfactory of all. At the same time, it must be recognized that if the text loses few of its specifically poetic values, this is because it probably lacked the most profound poetic values in the first place. One thing we really mean when we say that Campion's lyrics cry out for music, or that Wagner's librettos are admirably constructed to fit his musical style, is that as pure poems or plays they are insufficiently interesting.

The situation is not essentially different when a poet writes a lyric or a play for someone else to set to music. True, he can hardly forecast the exact reading the composer will choose, but if he is sensitive he will make sure that his poem reflects the use to which it will be put. He is unlikely to make it a vehicle for closely reasoned argument or subtle figures of speech if he suspects that they will later be sacrificed to the musical flow. Thus, in such lyrics as "It was a lover and his lass" and "When that I was and a little tiny boy" Shakespeare foregoes his usual complex pentameters with their tightly packed imagery in favor of simple stanza forms in which logic and even syntax are less important than sound and sentiment. And the good librettist will flatten out the characters in such plays as *Othello* and *The Marriage of Figaro*, neutralizing their verbal personalities, for he knows that the composer must embrace them all in a single inclusive musical style within which he can endow them with a new vocal individuality. Lyric and dramatic texts like these are already prepared for the composer's use and hence suffer minor dislocation when he takes them over.

Sometimes the union of words and music seems closer still. In many popular songs, and presumably in true folk songs as well, the composer has produced words and music as it were simultaneously. Furthermore, we are led to believe that some poet-and-composer teams work so closely together that their products can also be considered as twin-born. In the best of these, from ballads to Beatles, the relation between music and text is similar to the one that obtains in the art song. But the required balance between the two components is evidently hard to maintain. Most of the popular favorites stemming from the twenties and thirties were primarily tunes: their words usually consisted of easily grasped clichés of rhymed sentimentality serving as vehicles for the melodies, which were the source of whatever distinction these songs possessed. Today, however, in many songs of the pseudofolk and other varieties, the situation is reversed: the music has become a vehicle for the projection of personal, social, or cosmic significance.

The use of music primarily to project important words is certainly not unknown in other contexts. Music plays this utilitarian role in psalmody and in recitative. And if the composer restricts the scope of his own voice in favor of complete textual clarity—or if, as I suspect of some of today's popular idols, he has never fully developed his own voice—the musical persona embodies a minimal transformation of the poetic. The composer's voice has assumed the task of projecting and amplifying that of the poet. (Today, unfortunately, the poet's voice is often amplified more in a literal than in a figurative sense.) This is the concept of song put forth by Goethe when he praised Zelter for setting his poems to music that, "like an inflow of gas, merely carries the balloon aloft."[1] But such an attitude has never satisfied composers for long; indeed, a common view of the history of opera sees it as a record of the varying resolutions of the conflict between the demands of the music for self-fulfillment and the needs of the text for projection and amplification.

In all the above cases, however, the composer remains in control, at least to the extent that it is he who decides what the balance shall be and thus determines the nature of the complete persona of the song. But sometimes, again especially in the realm of popular music, a poet writes words for music previously composed. Now the composer's control is seriously challenged. Even if the music was written in the expectation of such use, it must still undergo considerable modification through the addition of the text. The sound of the words and their articulation is bound to make some difference in the phrasing of the melody, and the sense of the poem particularizes the implied mood of the music. The musical persona may remain predominant, but it is no longer that of the composer alone. It is the hybrid offspring of the original composer and the poet, and it is no less a hybrid if the same man performs both functions. The musical transformation is even more striking when previously composed music is given words that it did not expect —whether new words to replace old ones (like Goethe's folk-song texts, and like the "Danny-Boys" and "apple blossoms" applied to the Londonderry Air), or words added to an in-

[1] Max Hecker, ed., *Der Briefwechsel zwischen Goethe und Zelter* (Leipzig: Insel-Verlag, 1913), Vol. II, p. 59.

strumental composition (like many recent travesties of familiar classics). In each case there is a distortion of the original musical values; it is especially severe when a vocal persona is introduced into an instrumental context.

It may be prejudice that insists that such examples produce hybrid personas. If a normally composed song transforms a previously independent poem into a component of the composer's voice, why does a song produced in the reverse manner not result in the subordination of the composer's statement to that of the poet? My reason is based on the conviction that, in most encounters between poetry and music, poetry can become the more powerful of the two only by virtue of the intentional acquiescence or the unintentional incompetence of the composer. If the music has already proved its independent viability, the composer's voice will almost inevitably be heard. To be sure, this is probably not the case when hymns or national anthems are derived from old tunes by the applications of new words, but here, as we shall see, one hardly attends to the music at all, regardless of its origin or its prior potentialities. Witty parodies, too, can force one to pay special attention to the words at the expense of the music. On the other hand, the prevalence of the hybrid persona is supported by the number of examples in which the substitution or addition of new words has been made, not for the sake of the poetry, but in order to increase the availability of the music or to enhance its commercial value. (In most of these, matters are complicated still further by the work of an arranger, so that the composer's voice is anything but pure—yet it is still strangely clear. The fact that we can recognize and acknowledge the presence of Chopin and Tchaikovsky in the popular versions of their melodies attests the indestructibility of the composer's persona.)

These problems are probably of little interest to the serious musician, but they are closely related to others with which he may well be concerned: those arising from translation, and from the use of strophic forms.

The translation of any literary text, even without reference to musical use, raises difficult questions as to the identity of the author's voice. Just who is speaking, the author's persona or the translator's? Obviously we are again dealing with a hybrid form, for two authors have contributed to the production of a single text. What might be called the legitimate translation tries, so far as possible, to subordinate the voice of the second author, so that the reader can hear the original author's voice behind and through the translator's. But there exists a class of translations, or, more properly, adaptations, in which the translator uses the text as a means of promoting his own persona. I am told that Edward FitzGerald's *Rubaiyat* is an example of this kind (as opposed, say, to Robert Fitzgerald's *Odyssey*). It is an example that indicates, however, that there is nothing morally or artistically reprehensible about this kind of appropriation, as long as one makes no false claims about its relationship to the original. (There is an interesting parallel between the translation of a text and the performance of a composition, although this analogy must not be pushed too far. To a certain extent, however, every performance, except sheer improvisation, is a joint product of composer and interpreter(s)—even when composer and interpreter are the same individual. And whereas the aim of legitimate performance should be the projection of the composer's persona, it is not uncommon for a performer to use a composition as a vehicle for the self-indulgent display of his own personality.)

No matter how faithfully a translation preserves the general form and the intellectual content of an original text, it must fail to retain the sound. At best, then, it is an uneasy mixture of the translator's (new) sound and the author's (paraphrased) sense. Consequently, the more important the sheer sound of a writer's voice is, the less his personality will emerge from the new version; and the more his sense actually depends on his sound, the more his works will resist translation of any kind.

The translation of a song, or of an opera, is a special case of a new poem fitted to preexisting music. Here, of course, the responsible translator does his best to preserve the bare meaning of the original, but the inevitable transformation of the verbal sound not only alters the poetic content but also distorts the musical values. And the musical distortion reflects back upon the poetic meaning as well. A tiny example, relevant even though it does not involve translation but only a revision of the composer's syllabication, is found in "Là ci darem la mano." In Zerlina's first response to the Don, her extension of his eight-measure period is initiated by the rise of her line through an arpeggiation to a repetition of the word "ma" on E, so that her delay of the cadence appears to be motivated by a realization of the implications of that crucial "but." In some performances, however, the soprano extends the word "ancor" throughout the arpeggiation, postponing "ma" in order to achieve an easier and smoother vocal climax—but by the same token sacrificing the intimate musico-verbal relationship of meaning (Ex. 5). If such a syllabic detail can thus affect the sense of a passage, how much more will a change of language! No matter how clever the translation may be, no matter how traditional or convenient or even necessary its use, it inevitably produces a hybrid form in which it is impossible to hear the composer's voice in its pure state. Of course when the composer himself works on the translated version, making the musical revisions necessary to adapt the vocal line to the new language, as in Gluck's Paris *Orphée* and *Alceste*, then once more the composer's voice is clear—but in a new composition. The new version and the old are closely

5. Mozart, *Don Giovanni*, "Là ci darem la mano." In m. 16 the revised prosody is given in parentheses.

related, but they are not the same opera. Such pairs of works might best be considered as variations of each other.

The principle of variation is at work in the strophic song, too, for each succeeding stanza can be heard as a variation of the first. This is one form in which the music is expressly designed to fit more than one set of words. Usually we have no way of knowing in a specific example which stanza was composed first or whether all were composed roughly at once, but this makes no difference in performance: we *hear* them one by one, from the first to the last, and thus we hear each later stanza as a modification of the first. And in examples by the great lieder composers—those from *Die schöne Müllerin*, for instance—a great deal of the interest of the form derives from the composer's ability to adapt a musical setting of highly individualized profile to diverse phonetic and semantic contexts through subtle transformations, sometimes in the manner of performance and sometimes in the musical substance itself. The process is thus variation rather than repetition, and the result is really a continuous form—a through-composed song that just happens to be strophic, so to speak.

There are, to be sure, many songs for which the strophic form is prescribed—hymns and ballads, for example—whose musical interest is not sufficiently high to maintain our attention throughout the required repetitions. Then we hear the music less as a theme with variations than as an unchanging background for the projection of a text, which is the real center of interest. Indeed, as I have already suggested, one hardly hears the music of a hymn at all.

Is it correct, though, to claim that the text is the center of interest of a hymn? If we hardly hear the music as we sing a hymn, are we any more conscious of the import of the words? Are not both music and words at the service of the ritual, of the occasion? The hymn is a good example of a class that I call *functional song*, to which dramatistic analysis does not apply. Functional song is a variety of what might be thought of as natural song—natural, that is, as opposed to artificial (or artistic, if you prefer). Now, one distinguishing mark of natural song is that its vocal persona is not a dramatic character: the persona is an aspect of the actual singer at the time of singing. In functional song, the singer expresses himself directly as a member of a specific community, engaged in performing a task, or taking part in a ritual, or assisting at a social event. Think, for example, of the occasions on which we sing "Happy Birthday to You." This useful composition is a paradigm of functional song. It marks the observation of a social form. Everyone who sings it means it, or pretends to mean it. No one imagines himself to be the poetic-vocal persona of the song—each person *is* the persona; and unlike a dramatic persona, this one is obviously conscious of singing. In the same way, no one ever thinks of the music as embodying a composer's voice, or indeed as having been composed at all.[2] The concept of a musical persona is irrelevant here, for the music is taken for granted as simply there to be used. Hence no one listens to the music—or to the words either, for that matter. The music exists in order to create a sense of unanimity in the projection of the words, and the words are used, not for their poetic value (which is nonexistent), or even for their meaning, but for their availability as ritual symbols.

This divorce of functional song from esthetic value, although common today, is nonetheless an aberration. There is no reason why functional music should not be of the highest quality, enjoyable as well as useful—and enjoyed as well as used. The fact that today it so seldom is enjoyable points to a decline in the general quality of life, as reflected in our present-day ceremonies and rituals. What Dewey has to say of artifacts is applicable to music as well:

That many, perhaps most, of the articles and utensils made at present for use are not genuinely esthetic happens, unfortunately, to be true. But it is true for reasons that are foreign to the relation of the "beautiful" and "useful" as such. Wherever conditions are such as to prevent the act of production from being an experience in which the whole creature is alive and in which he possesses his living through enjoyment, the product will lack something of being esthetic. No matter how useful it is for special and limited ends, it will not be useful in the ultimate degree—that of contributing directly and liberally to an expanding and enriched life.[3]

Hymns, to be sure, often contain both words and music of superlative quality, representing functional song at its best: enjoyable to sing, and at the same time rewarding to listen to. As a result their esthetic value has survived the uses to which they have been put. For, qua hymns, they are not full-fledged

---

[2] It *was* composed, however—by Mildred J. Hill (1859–1916).

[3] John Dewey, *Art as Experience* (New York: Minton, Balch, 1934), pp. 26–27.

works of art. Their tunes are not necessarily associated with a single set of words; in many hymnals these tunes are classified by meters in order to facilitate new associations of music and text. Their style is determined by the exigencies of congregational performance and by the conventions of local piety. Their accompaniments are simple, for the most part doubling the vocal lines. It was with good reason that the Puritans banned instruments from their churches. Their presence might have tempted composers to write independent parts for them, and in so doing turn functional music into art music—making a dramatic performance out of what ought to be an act of individual and congregational worship.

For hymns can become works of art. They can be sung for their own sake, and heard with pleasure. In principle any functional song can undergo this change of status, provided it possesses a modicum of artistic quality. One need only perform it in a situation that demands esthetic attention rather than, or in addition to, active participation. It then ceases to be a purely functional song and becomes, at least in part, the dramatic simulation of one. And so we have seasonal programs in which Christmas carols are solemnly presented on the same platform with complex polyphonic choruses by Bach and Handel. Fortunately, some of them are good enough to survive such treatment.

Music can also move in the opposite direction. Old tunes are sometimes given new words in order to adapt them to a spurious social function. Thus "Greensleeves" can become a familiar Christmas carol, and Beethoven's "Ode to Joy" a hymn celebrating the Common Market.

Today most functional song is rigidly conventional in form. Its expressiveness, even when not minimal, is usually highly generalized; that is, the music relates, not to the specific words with which it happens to be associated, but to a broadly defined attitude, social or religious in nature. That is no doubt the reason why it is easy for "God Save the King" to become "America." (One should perhaps not enquire too closely into the rationale that transforms "To Anacreon in Heaven" into "The Star-Spangled Banner.") Yet such functional song may represent the last vestige in our artificial society of a natural song of personal and spontaneous expression: a persuasive or rhetorical song, possibly improvised for the occasion, in which, for example, the singer propitiates the Deity, or woos a beloved, or puts a baby to sleep. Natural song of this kind would arise from expressive intent, for presumably it could not persuade if it were not expressive. Furthermore, it could not persuade if it were not listened to (though a lullaby is successful only when it is no longer being heard!). In this respect it differs from conventionally functional song, whose efficacy depends, not on the persuasive powers of the music, but merely on the addressee's realization that the performance is taking place.

Rhetorical song is not art, if by art we mean the intentional production of objects for disinterested contemplation. Song of this kind has a specific job to do, and it arises as a practical response to an immediate situation. But like the hymn it can become art: the natural song can be lifted out of its context, performed on the concert stage, and listened to by an audience. At that point it is no longer natural: it has become a simulation, and the singer is now engaged in a dramatic impersonation. That is what happens when Marian Anderson sings "Swing Low, Sweet Chariot": she recreates, as a dramatic persona, the slave who originally sang it as an authentic appeal. Simulations of this kind result in a dramatic vocal persona that *is* conscious of singing—for that is part of its role.

The vocal protagonist created in this way must be distinguished from another type, illustrated by Albert Hay Malotte's "The Lord's Prayer." The words of this syrupy concoction, qua prayer, do not normally constitute a dramatic utterance. Spoken prayers are meant to express the actual or pretended feelings of the worshipper who pronounces them; versified, they are often set as hymns. But Malotte, in turning the Lord's Prayer into a kind of concert aria, has made of it a dramatic performance. The singer is not praying but enacting a character who is praying. There is nothing intrinsically wrong with the use of a sacred text for such a purpose; unfortunately, the character portrayed in this example is a repulsively sentimental type who addresses the Deity in a cloyingly mawkish manner. This protagonist is appropriately supported by an accompaniment that underlines every gesture with clichés of conventional religiosity or of exaggerated emotionalism. As a result, the implicit persona inferred by the musically alert is quite different from the one demanded by the connotations of the text and hence naturally assumed by those who devote their pious attention primarily to the words. The listener who is as sensitive to musical as to verbal values will turn gratefully to the dignity and the relative impersonality of Stravinsky's "Pater noster."

Love songs, especially serenades such as Schubert's well-known "Ständchen" from *Schwanengesang*, might be assumed to simulate what was once a natural song type; at least, by their rhetoric that is what they claim to do, for they create the dramatic situation of an importunate lover wooing his lady through song. Here again, apparently, is the dramatic impersonation of a character in a situation naturally calling for song. But is this really the case? Is there actually such a thing as a love song, outside the conventions of the love song itself? From the troubadours on, the love song was a literary genre depending on the creation of an often highly artificial persona, so even when it was employed as a means of real wooing (if indeed it ever was), it must have involved a strong element of self-dramatization. Such a song as the Schubert "Ständchen," then, presents a double level of impersonation, for the character portrayed in Schubert's song is a serenade singer, who in turn wears his own mask. We might say that a song like Schubert's does simulate a natural love song, but a hypothetical one that may never have really existed.

A more obvious example of impersonation is to be found in Don Giovanni's serenade. Of course the Don wishes the object of his intentions to hear him as singing a naturally rhetorical song, but we know that he has carefully developed an artificial persona in order to gain his amatory ends. In this case, indeed, the persona is more than artificial: it is false, for the Don is disguising himself as his servant, Leporello. But if I am right, this impersonation is only an exaggeration of the underlying strategy of all love song, no matter how lofty in tone or intent.

Rhetorical song of another type is simulated by both Monteverdi and Gluck when Orfeo stands at the gates of Hades. Both composers dramatically present the hero as trying to win over the guardians of hell by his vocal powers. (Monteverdi makes the simulation clear by the vocal display; Gluck, by the accompanying harp.) I should like to go even further and suggest that "Che farò" may not be what it is usually taken to be, an aria in which the character directly expresses his grief, but perhaps—at least on one level—a performance: not an aria but an "aria," consciously "sung" by the character in his profession as musician. He has won his way past the Furies with his powers of song; why would he not try to persuade the gods themselves to relent? Thus "Che farò" would be Orfeo's "Voi che sapete" rather than his "Non so più": a "song" specially composed—on the spot, to be sure, but Orfeo would be equal to the task! Such a view would go far toward explaining why the aria is more notable for its abstract beauty than for its depth of expression. I grant that this interpretation finds little support in the libretto, which stresses the power of love, but surely the effect of the opera is to celebrate the power of music.

Most types of functional and other natural song, whether actual or simulated, display one common feature: they are addressed to someone or something: to the Deity, to one's fellow, to one's country, to one's beloved. There is one category of which this is not true: pure natural song expressing simple emotions—singing for joy, singing for sorrow. Some folk songs, especially some spirituals, realize this possibility, and so do some contemporary forms of community singing.

This natural genre, too, is imitated by more artificial forms of poetry and music. Some lyrics call for a simple and straightforward musical setting that would simulate natural, unmediated vocal expression. For example, the first poem of *Die schöne Müllerin*, "Das Wandern," might be read as the utterance of a young man who is not just enjoying life, but consciously *singing for joy*. Schubert's song could accordingly be heard as a simulation of natural expressive singing. An interpretation of this kind, applied to a number of the songs in this cycle, would explain their emphasis on simple melodies and strophic forms: these songs represent not merely the thoughts of the protagonist, but songs composed (improvised) by him.

The brook, too, seems to be a composer. Addressed as a friend by the hero in a number of the lyrics, it comes to life dramatically in "Der Müller und der Bach"; and the last song, "Des Baches Wiegenlied," is fancifully presented as a lullaby composed and sung by the brook itself. But has Schubert presented here the mere simulation of a natural cradle song? Surely there is a second or even third level of impersonation implied: the brook is not singing in its own guise, but is itself simulating a mother who sings her child to sleep—and the brook, as the vocal unity of the cycle attests, is in turn only the projection of the hero's gloomy imagination. What we hear, then, is not a natural lullaby nor the simulation of one, but the dramatic portrayal of the imagined simulation of a lullaby. Whatever the implications of the poem, Schubert's magical accompaniment clearly equates the lapping of the waves with the rocking of the cradle, and the melodic line is closely connected with earlier ones unequivocally assigned to the hero. (Compare, for example, the concluding vocal cadences of this song and of "Trockne Blumen": Ex. 6.) The music stands as a

6. Schubert, songs from *Die schöne Müllerin*.

constant reminder that behind the image of the mother, evoked by the singing brook that personifies the despondent mood of the hero, we must infer a consciousness whose thought can evoke and control all the relationships in a song of such complex simplicity. It is, of course, the consciousness implied by the interaction of word, voice, and accompaniment throughout the song cycle: its implicit musical persona.

4

Text and Texture: Song
and Performance

The examples so far adduced to explain and justify the notions of the vocal protagonist and the composer's implicit persona may have encouraged the suspicion that these concepts, if they have any relevance at all, apply only to cases where a single voice (or an ensemble of single voices) is supported by an instrumental accompaniment. It is true that it is easier to accept the image of the vocal protagonist when it is personified by a solo performer; and it is also true that the pervasiveness of a fairly elaborate accompaniment, embodying what I have called a virtual persona of its own, helps us first to keep the implicit persona distinct from that of the voice alone, and then to follow the thread of its discourse. But neither solo performance nor instrumental accompaniment is necessary. The only requisite is the integrity of the musical line. By way of emphasizing this important point, I have sometimes called the implicit persona of the composition the *complete musical persona*. This locution also reminds us that the persona is by no means identical with the composer; it is a projection of his musical intelligence, constituting the mind, so to speak, of the composition in question. (Strictly speaking, in a song the persona should be called the poetic-musical persona, to indicate the composer's appropriation of the text. But the shorter form is more convenient, and it is applicable to purely instrumental music as well.)

When a song lacks accompaniment, the musical and the vocal personas coincide. In a sense they become identical; yet for purposes of analysis we can still usually distinguish between them, for we can look at the single persona from two points of view. The typical protagonist, we remember, is assumed to be actually unconscious of singing. Not so the implicit musical persona, which is always aware of both words and music; the musical persona is an intelligence in the act of thinking through words and music alike. The distinction becomes clear if we realize that, in the absence of an accompanist, the *singer*, who is, or ought to be, completely aware of every aspect of the song, can be thought of as representing the implicit musical persona; the *persona portrayed by the singer within the song* is the vocal protagonist. Or, to return to two old friends, the protagonist is the voice of Caliban in Browning's poem; the implicit persona is Browning's voice, speaking through Caliban.

There are other cases where, for all practical purposes, musical and vocal personas coincide, even in the presence of an accompaniment. The instrumental part may consist of a single line doubling the voice. The troubadours may well have accompanied themselves, or had themselves accompanied, in this way. Hardly more independent is the instrumental part that, while consisting of simple chords rather than pure melodic doubling, is essentially nothing more than an amplification of the vocal line, as in the accompaniments devised by balladeers for performance on lute, guitar, harp, or the like.

All these are examples of what I call *simple song*: song with no accompaniment at all or with "simple" accompaniment— that is, accompaniment that has no individuality. Such an instrumental part, lacking the independence to claim a component persona of its own, should ideally be performed by the singer himself, as an extension of his own part. If he must relegate it to a second person, this accompanist, if sensitive, will do his best to minimize his own presence and to create the effect of the single, "simple" performer.

Many otherwise simple accompaniments contain brief

preludes, interludes, and postludes. So long as these are primarily functional, helping the singer to find his pitch and allowing him to rest after each stanza, they can be considered further natural extensions of the voice part. But if these passages take on a life of their own, the accompaniment ceases to be simple and assumes its own persona. If the singer persists in accompanying himself under such circumstances, he is trying to force the protagonist's psyche to envelop and take over that persona. Sometimes this can be successfully accomplished, especially if the accompaniment is not assertively independent; for, after all, one of its functions is to reveal aspects of the protagonist's subconscious. On the other hand, the result is often a severe dramatic strain that parallels the technical strain to which the singer must inevitably subject himself in carrying out the double task.

The fact that simple song projects a single persona—a protagonist who in fact or in theory produces his own accompaniment—allows it on occasion to convey the impression that the singer is improvising both words and music, whether or not this is really the case. Thus not only is simple song the obvious medium for natural song of all kinds, but it is also ideal for producing a simulation of natural song. In natural song the concepts of poet and composer are hardly relevant: there is only a musician singing on an occasion calling for musical expression. The simulation of natural song attempts to portray such an occasion.

Another category of simple song, the true ballad, reflects a different situation: the narration of a traditional tale by a storyteller, presumably in response to the demands of an audience, formal or informal, large or small. But our present-day balladeers, in contradistinction to those of old, are actors—though not in the manner of lieder singers who perform Schubert's or Loewe's dramatic "ballads." To be sure, an accomplished balladeer will not fail to do justice to the dramatic aspects of the traditional ballads, but his primary impersonation is not to be found *within* the texts of these songs at all. His is a second-level portrayal: he enacts the storyteller, not the persona of the story told. The sophisticated modern ballad singer is playing the part of a true ballad singer.

Occasionally he may go further. Simple song, in the absence of an independent accompaniment, is often able to absorb a good deal of elaboration and variation in performance. In the presentation of a ballad, such modifications, especially if improvised on the spot, lend a convincing verisimilitude to the fiction that the song is being composed for the occasion. In this case the balladeer impersonates, not a mere storyteller, but a poet-composer in the act of casting his story into a uniquely memorable form.

Some types of fully accompanied song, notably the baroque aria, likewise permit improvisation, mostly in the form of additional ornaments and cadenzas. From an operatic point of view the desired effect ought to be that the character, not the singer, is "composing" the aria, producing a subconscious musical response to a specific dramatic situation. In historical practice the singer often took over, seizing every opportunity for vocal display. The resulting excesses produced what Gluck and others considered an undramatic degeneration of the opera seria that called for a thoroughgoing reform.

Not all musical styles can stand even judicious elaboration on the part of the performer, and it is often difficult to decide just where, and to what extent, it is permissible. These problems, however, are only an exaggerated form of those inherent in all arts of performance. A singer, like an actor, is both a dramatic character and a real person. As a character, he must move in accordance with the prescriptions of the musico-dramatic situation—that is, he must be faithful to the text. But as a person, he must insist on his own freedom of action—that is, he must produce his own interpretation of that text. The tension between these two aspects of the singer's role thus curiously parallels the one we have already noted within the dramatic character he portrays: the tension between his tendencies toward freedom as a "person" and the restrictions upon him as an artistic motif. Whenever we see a play, whenever we hear an opera, and indeed, whenever we listen to a song, we are, or should be, aware of the force of these tensions. Presenting as they do analogues of the tension between freedom and determinism that most of us feel operative in our own lives, they may explain the peculiar appeal of the arts of performance.

The tension can break down, however, as the result of an illegitimate but all too common type of performance: that in which the singer displays an inappropriate awareness of his audience. For just as an operatic character, for example, must appear to be unaware of his accompaniment, or of the very act of singing, so the dramatic situation normally requires him to seem unaware of the presence of an audience. Sometimes, as we have seen, this rule is deliberately violated, as in the Prologue to *Pagliacci,* and there are occasions when convention allows or requires the characters to sing directly to the audience, as in the finale of *The Rake's Progress.* Indiscriminate indulgence in this kind of behavior, however, has been common in the history of opera, and it inevitably destroys the dramatic illusion by calling attention to the person of the performer at the expense of the character he is enacting.

Although such destruction of the dramatic illusion is perhaps most egregious in a theatrical setting, it is by no means restricted to opera. Similar unfortunate results can obtain even when a concert singer or a balladeer properly directs his performance toward the audience. There is a subtle but clear distinction between the legitimate inclusion of the listeners in the dramatic ambiance of a song and the exploitation of their relation to the singer in order to enhance his personal glory.

The legitimate interpretation, the "faithful" performance for which every singer should strive, is the one in which the two aspects of person and persona fuse. The physical presence and the vitality of the singer turn the persona of the poetic-musical text into an actual, immediate, living being: the *person* of the singer invests the *persona* of the song with *personality*. If the impersonation is successful, if the illusion is complete, we hear this embodied persona as "composing" his part—as living through the experience of the song. The vocal persona may be of various kinds—protagonist, character, etc., but, barring the unlikely possibility that we now ever witness the actual creation of natural song by its composer-performer, the persona is never identical with the singer.

The illegitimate interpretation is the one in which not the vocal persona but the singer—Mr. X or Miss Y there on the stage—becomes the "composer," the experiencing subject of the song. Eliot's comment on the dramatic monologue comes once more to mind here. The faithful performance, like Shakespeare's Caliban, allows us to hear the persona, and hence the composer's voice behind the persona, speak for itself. The illegitimate interpretation, like Browning's Caliban, forces us to hear the singer speaking through the persona and hence converting the composer's voice into a medium for his own self-expression. (This misappropriation can occur even when a singer performs songs of his own composition, if—as is often the case with pop singers—the emphasis is entirely on the immediate performance. I do not mean to imply that there is anything morally, or even esthetically, wrong about this practice. I merely insist that what one is listening to in such cases—as in many virtuoso performances of "serious" music—is not the piece be-ing performed, but the performance itself.)

The independent instrumental accompaniment is the me-dium through which the musical persona speaks directly, with-out the intervention of the vocal component. By the same token, its successful performance produces the impression that its music is being composed, or thought, not so much *by* as *through* the accompanist. For, unlike the singer, he is not en-acting the role of a "real" persona; he is symbolically conveying the presence of a virtual persona. Thus he should never assert his own personality in the way that a singer can and must; yet it is through his individual vitality that the virtual persona comes to life. If he is successful, he will produce the effect of a spon-taneity that seems to inhere, not in his own activity, but in that of the music itself. The music will then appear to live its own life, so to speak—to compose or to think through itself.

In opera, and in other forms that combine voices with an elaborate orchestral accompaniment, the presence of the con-ductor adds yet another level of complexity. He is, so to speak, the surrogate of the implicit persona—or ought to be, for he, too, is subject to a tension between person and persona that is sometimes resolved in favor of his own personality. Ideally, however, he turns the persona's demands on behalf of a unified construct into actual commands. The singers must obey; yet neither they nor the characters they impersonate must appear to give up their freedom. (The extent to which an analogous rule applies to the instrumentalists will be discussed in connec-tion with purely orchestral music.) The most satisfactory solu-tion is found when the singers do not give up their freedom but freely do what the conductor enjoins, thus affording a visible and audible symbol of the relationship between the characters and the musical persona that controls them. (The singer's atti-tude may be compared to that of the believer who strives to will freely the Will of God.) It is just as well, perhaps, that the conductor's position in the pit allows us most of the time to overlook his presence and to forget his insistent beat. The more visible he is, the less individualized the characters can be, and the less we can submit to the dramatic illusion. I suspect that this is one reason why most concert performances of opera are so unsatisfying.

On the concert stage the dramatic illusion is often under attack from another quarter. If a lieder singer impersonates a protagonist, if an accompanist tries to create an effect of spontaneity, how can we tolerate—as we often must—their use of scores? Isn't the illusion bound to fail under these circumstances? Oddly enough, the illusion does not fail, even under apparently more difficult conditions. "Readings" of plays, in which the characters openly read their parts from script, are often effective, and oratorio performances, with no semblance of staging or acting, can be dramatically convincing. To a certain extent such success is due to the familiarity of the convention: we accept these modes of performance and in a sense overlook them. But I think there is a deeper reason for our acquiescence. The physical presence of the score (or of its parts) is a constant reminder—for both performers and audience—of the control of the complete musical persona. In this respect the visible score is not unlike the figure of the conductor. The use of the score threatens the illusion of spontaneity, but at the same time it inhibits the excessive liberty that turns a composition into a vehicle for the performer's self-expression or virtuosity. When we attend a play reading, we are probably more interested in the construction of the whole, and in the author's message, than in the specific portrayals. In the same way, concert performances of operas with highly individualized characters are less likely to be tolerable than those of oratorios, or oratoriolike operas, in which the emphasis is on narrative continuity and abstract musical structures. In these instances it is less important to maintain the fiction of individual freedom than to assert the primacy of the all-inclusive persona.

In the performance of solo song, it is common practice for a pianist, reading the score, to accompany a singer who performs from memory. Aside from matters of practical convenience, this arrangement offers the advantage of visually emphasizing the two differing roles: the actual vocal persona of the singer and the virtual instrumental persona of the accompanist. Indeed, no one who keeps in mind the symbolic nature of instrumental performance in general need ever be disturbed by a player's use of notes. If they inhibit spontaneity, it is the personal spontaneity of the player, not the inherent spontaneity of the music, that suffers. And since the two often come into conflict, it is sometimes fortunate that the presence of the score can remind the performer where his primary loyalty should reside.

If singing and playing from score need not destroy the dramatic illusion, this is especially true in cases where the characterization requires no high degree of personal specificity, as in choral singing. Here again the score, in addition to offering obvious conveniences, can serve advantageously as a continual reminder to each member of the choir of his duties to his vocal section, and of the relation of that section to the whole. The freedom of every choral singer is severely limited, and the score—again like the conductor—is a visible symbol of this circumscription.

At the same time a chorus has a dramatic role to play; and so, accordingly, does every member of it. Each of them, however, should be thought of not as a persona (that is, a protagonist or character) in his own right, but rather as one member of what might be called a multiple persona: a group in which each member foregoes his individuality to take part in a common enterprise. In unison singing, plainsong for example, the entire choir constitutes one multiple persona, representing the body of worshippers. The same is probably true of simple chordal part singing, in which each part can still be heard as a component of one persona. More complicated polyphonic settings, however, divide the chorus into what must be perceived as two or more multiple personas, often in dramatic dialogue or even conflict with one another.

In this connection, it is puzzling to understand how one is meant to hear the polytextual and even sometimes polylingual Gothic motet. Here the several personas, different as they are both verbally and musically, are by no means in dramatic conflict with one another. They are in no way involved with one another; in fact, to maintain the dramatistic point of view we must say that they are entirely unaware of one another.

Perhaps these motets were hardly ever performed for an audience, being written primarily for the enjoyment of sophisticated singers and players. Or perhaps, if there was an audience, its members were expected to hear the work in diverse ways, depending on their familiarity with the languages, the texts, and the musical materials. Still, one wants to make the most complete sense of these compositions that one can; so the best solution may be the one suggested by Lang:

[The Gothic motet] required from the listener a new approach and a new conception of listening to music, for . . . [it] did not establish an intimate relationship between listener and singer. Instead of concentrating on a group of singers, the listener had to follow three individual parts presenting three distinct moods. . . . The listener . . . must make his choice, select a part and follow it, and then become a part of the polyphonic web.[1]

[1] Paul Henry Lang, *Music in Western Civilization* (New York: Norton, 1941), p. 147.

Lang seems to imply here that such a motet is really not one composition but three, depending on which voice one follows. In each case that voice becomes the main one; the other two, its accompaniment. (The tenor, in some instances at least, may have been purely instrumental, and then only two texts would actually have been heard. But the tenor could still carry with it the associations of its original words, which could presumably be rehearsed mentally by one familiar with them.)

Where is the composer's voice to be heard in such a composition, if one listens to it as Lang suggests? Perhaps the answer must be that it is not *heard* in the sense that we are now accustomed to; instead of being inferred from the progression of the whole, it can only be intellectually reconstructed from the relationships between the individual musical lines and the texts they set. An examination of these relationships might reveal, for example, the composer's intention, devout or ironic, in choosing just those components. One may complain that this music requires an intellectualistic approach to what should be a basically sensuous experience, but similar criticisms have been applied to other aspects of Gothic art as well.[2]

The association of musical parts asserting or implying a multiplicity of texts continues long after the death of the Gothic motet, into the cantus firmus, paraphrase, and parody techniques of the Renaissance. When these techniques are used, the source material can almost always be considered as an abstract musical motif, without regard for its original text; the composer's voice comes through clearly enough in those terms. In many cases he himself probably thought of his source in that way—or are we to assume that every composer using "L'homme armé" had its words in mind? But at other times the words associated with the musical material comment on the overt text

[2] See, for example, Wylie Sypher, *Four Stages of Renaissance Style* (Garden City: Doubleday, 1956), pp. 36–55.

or on the circumstances of composition and performance—as may have been the case with Josquin's "La Sol Fa Re Mi." Once again, this kind of content could have yielded its secrets only to extra-musical analysis.

None of the above examples should be confused with the practice of *dramatic* polytextuality, in which each musical part represents a dramatic role. Thus Bach, although using the old cantus firmus technique in the opening chorus of the *St. Matthew Passion*, put it to the service of a vividly realized theatrical conception. The two main choirs ("Kommt, ihr Töchter") portray the women of Jerusalem; the additional sopranos (the chorale), the devout Christians whose meditations have summoned up the mystical vision of the Crucifixion. As the uniqueness of its melody and text makes clear, this choir exists on a different plane of action from the others, who are taking part in the events to be narrated. I have heard a performance of this work, with apparent historical justification, in which the chorale was not sung, but assigned to the organ. No matter: presumably the tune was so well known to Bach's audience that it alone was sufficient to recall the words. Bach was careful to introduce each phrase of this melody, and hence its explicit or implicit text, during passages of verbal repetition on the part of the principal choruses. The careful listener could turn his attention to the meaning of each new line of the chorale as it appeared; he could thus assimilate both texts during the performance without having to rely on a later mental reconstruction. Finally, the relation between the two planes of action is convincingly expounded by the musical form. Appearing at first to promise an alternation of double-fugato expositions with episodes of dialogue, the movement is soon revealed to be a huge chorale setting: the chorale calls into being the entire musical structure, just as the worshippers it symbolizes call forth, through their vision, the biblical scene.

It must be admitted that there are many examples in which the composer has apparently not yielded to the demands of dramatic propriety—compositions, say, in which a soloist may stand for a multitude of people, or in which a chorus may represent an individual. Sometimes even this practice may make a dramatic point, as when Schoenberg, in *Moses und Aron*, symbolizes the superpersonality of God by assigning His voice to a complex combination of solos and chorus, of singing and *Sprechstimme*, or when Stravinsky, in *The Flood*, gives it to two solo basses. But what dramatic point could Schütz have intended in his *Auferstehung* when he set as duets the voice, not only of Jesus, who might thus be distinguished from mere mortals, but also of Mary Magdalen?

One possible answer appears if we consider the nature of liturgies and other sacred texts. Insofar as we understand and accept these as received texts, we do not expect one speaking or singing them to assume a dramatic role. If he assumes a role at all, it is a ritual one, as when a priest becomes a celebrant. We imagine the singer of a received text not as "composing" new words but as reading or reciting traditional ones.

If the ritual is complete, we accept the music as equally traditional. That brings us back to functional song, which can be concisely defined as completely ritual song, of which both words and music are "given," that is, determined by some rite, religious or secular. From this point of view, "Happy Birthday to You" and Gregorian chant are equally "sacred" and equally functional. Only when we listen to Gregorian chant as music, not merely accepting it as part of the liturgy, do its esthetic values become important. In this case, even though we still assume that the text is ritually prescribed, we are listening to the music as if it were the (subconscious) expression of a vocal persona. But the persona is to be imagined as *repeating* or *reading* the text, not as living through it.

This way of hearing Gregorian chant is one model for the esthetic apprehension, as opposed to the ritual acceptance, of any music composed for liturgical or other sacred texts. We hear the music as expressive, and hence as embodying the sub-conscious attitudes of a protagonist, but the protagonist is the devout Bible reader, or worshipper, or celebrant. Thus we can hear Josquin's "Absalon, fili mi," not as a dramatic representation of David's despair, but as the reaction of a reader, or group of readers, to the Bible story. Hence the multiple persona of its choral setting, while dramatically improper, is not inappropriate. In the same way, Schütz's double Magdalen and double Christ might reflect the inclination of the devout reader to view those characters in a special light, to dwell on their words with a special attention symbolized by the relatively elaborate musical realization. Figures of this sort, set off from the musical context yet not fully realized as actual characters, might be thought of as quasi-dramatic: imagined so vividly by the vocal persona that they take on a life of their own. Late versions of the Requiem, such as those of Berlioz and Verdi, contain many movements that might best be thought of in this way. But it is neither easy nor necessary to decide just where this kind of "reading" stops and true drama begins. Does the soprano solo of Verdi's "Libera me" represent a vivid figure imagined by an impressionable worshipper, or is it the anguished cry of a dying soul? Has the liturgical text become for Verdi another opera libretto? Probably the truth is that Verdi could not help turning ritual into drama. The protagonist who presumably began by reading, or reciting, or contemplating the Requiem Mass surrendered to the power of his (her) own imagination (as symbolized by Verdi's overwhelming music) and actually assumed the role of the soul about to face its judgment. Verdi has often been criticized for his theatricality in this work, for his confusion of liturgy with opera. But what he achieved, after all—granted the distance between the styles—is not so different from Josquin's intense realization of David's lament or from Bach's dramatization of the Passion. For "Absalon" may be thought of as representing a group of readers, each of whom not only sympathetically repeats the words of David, but, going one step further, imaginatively identifies himself with the biblical figure. And Bach, through his chorales on the one hand and his arias on the other, suggests the constant presence of the devout reader who, both as a member of the congregation (in the chorales) and as an individual (in the arias), imagines the biblical scenes so vividly that they come to life before his eyes.

Bach's use of the chorale, not only here but in the cantatas as well, musically symbolizes the intermingling of ritual and drama underlying his most powerful conceptions. Like a Gregorian cantus firmus in a Renaissance motet or mass, the chorale melody, together with its text, is a ritual element because both its words and its music are traditional. But Bach's settings, like the polyphonic elaborations of the Renaissance cantus firmus, are original. In both, the multiple protagonist is a body of worshippers who, while accepting the traditional form (chorale or cantus firmus), think about it, comment on it, modify it. Bach's elaborate harmonizations and the independent instrumental parts that are often an integral part of his settings can be taken as referring to the subconscious attitudes of his multiple protagonist. Thus a chorale as performed in a cantata was not a real but a simulated hymn, taking its place as a component movement in a composition that, although an integral part of the church service, nevertheless produced its effect as a work of musico-dramatic art. At the same time, the ritual nature of its origin was not forgotten—at least by those members of the congregation who joined in the singing of the chorale melody. Provided they did so discreetly, without doing violence to the specific setting devised for the cantata in question, they did not deprive the chorale of its newly won artistic status, but rather added a dimension of true functionality to its simulated functionality, for they were the actual believers whom the choir represented. The chorale thus served in a double capacity: as an artistic motif within the cantata for the congregation to listen to, and as a ritually defined hymn for them to sing. (In this connection Berlioz's explanation of the presence of a third choir in addition to the double chorus of his *Te Deum* is interesting: this choir "represents the people adding their voice from time to time to the great ceremony of sacred music."[3] So do Bach's chorales.)

There is one form of song whose masterpieces have often been praised for being to a high degree both expressive and dramatic, not only in their text settings but also in their harmonic techniques, yet at the same time display an undeniable discrepancy between the meaning of their words and the method of their performance. For the many-voiced setting of the Renaissance madrigal often seems to belie the personal and even private nature of its text. We can accept a multiple persona for Morley's convivial "Sing we and chaunt it," but what about Monteverdi's polyphonic version of "Arianna's Lament," not to speak of the numerous love lyrics with which the literature, both English and Italian, abounds? There are several possible approaches to the problem, by no means mutually exclusive. Not all of them will apply to every example of the literature, complex and varied as it is. And although they may not all prove to be equally acceptable, they share the merit of obviating an explanation of the anomaly that relies on the excuse of pure convention.

First of all, a polyphonic setting does not necessarily imply a performance by several singers. Many madrigals could well be,

---

[3] David Cairns, trans., *The Memoirs of Hector Berlioz* (London: Gollancz, 1969), p. 479.

and probably often were, realized by a soloist with instrumental accompanists; and in the more elaborately polyphonic settings, it would have been almost a matter of indifference which line was chosen as the vocal one. I mention this possibility, not to recommend it as an ideal method of performance, but to indicate that the madrigal could be so conceived. Because of the uniformity of musical material and texture, any voice could be considered as representing the protagonist. Thus in an *a cappella* performance each singer could, if he chose, think of himself in this light, and of his colleagues as personifying the projections of his own psyche. A listener, too, could choose his protagonist, presumably the voice that most clearly presented itself as the musical leader of the ensemble.

A more abstruse way of interpreting the madrigal preserves the concept of the single vocal persona, but at the expense of the individual character. The vocal persona is now an abstraction, a construct deduced from the musical form itself rather than from any of the voices that contribute to it. The vocal persona not only coincides with but is essentially identical with the implicit musical persona. The singers do not "compose" their parts, but perform, almost like instruments, in the service of this overriding musical persona, which animates them and directs their thoughts. Unlike the components of a multiple persona, these singers individually have no realistic dramatic significance. They coalesce into a single abstract vocal persona representing what might be described more accurately as the entire poem than as the persona of the poem. And given the highly artificial nature of many of the texts used, in which the poetic persona often appears to be merely an excuse for the assertion of a paradox or the elaboration of a metaphor, this interpretation of the madrigal may often be appropriate.

A more generally satisfactory understanding of the madrigal, however, is based on the proposition that whenever there is a serious dramatic discrepancy between the meaning of a text and the prescribed method of its performance, one is meant to take the words, at least, as precomposed. We have already seen this principle at work in ritual, where the singer is assumed to be reciting a received text; now it is to be applied to nontraditional poems. The persona portrayed by a madrigal singer does not "compose"—does not live through—the words, but *reads* them. For the ensemble, as for the audience (if there is one), the poem is a literary creation which the singers read to themselves or to one another. Through the music they absorb it, savor it, comment on it, exaggerate it, play with it. A dramatic situation is thus created, but it is a highly artificial one, outside and around the text rather than within it: the singers impersonate the participants in a poetry reading.

A further step is possible here as in the case of "Absalon." A sensitive reader can not only interpret and comment on a poem as he reads it but also imaginatively assume the role of its protagonist; just so can each member of a madrigal group be thought of as portraying such a reader. There will thus be a double level of impersonation, each singer playing the part of a reader who imagines himself as the protagonist.

Contrast, for example, Monteverdi's two versions of "Arianna's Lament." The solo protagonist is Arianna herself, reacting directly to her situation in the drama. In the madrigal, no member of the ensemble can be construed as *being* Arianna, but all sympathetically share her emotions as they read and discuss the text. The material of their discussion might even be thought of as including the original monody as well: they try to intensify its expression by exaggerating its chromaticism. In so doing, each of them might well assume the role of Arianna in imagination, privately reliving her experiences. The subtly complex expressive content resulting from these various levels of activity parallels the complication of the polyphony; so, effective as such a madrigal undeniably is, it is easy to understand why the monodists thought of themselves as turning toward a more natural and realistic form of musico-dramatic expression.

The concept of performance as reading a poem rather than directly assuming a dramatic role is occasionally applicable to the solo art song too, especially when the setting is simple enough to invite self-accompaniment. Thus the protagonist of Beethoven's *Sechs geistliche Lieder* Op. 48 might be thought of as reading or reciting prayers—or even singing hymns. In all but the last of the group, the vocal line is straightforward and unadorned. The piano part asserts no independence; its function is to double the voice and to harmonize its melody. These are basically "simple" songs, and they may well have been designed for private devotional use.

The madrigal is of course essentially unaccompanied; when instruments are used at all, they double or replace vocal parts. As in simple song, there is no independent instrumental persona. In contradistinction, the instrumental doublings frequently prescribed for the vocal parts of post-Renaissance choral music may assume roles of their own. True, they can sometimes be dismissed as mere utility parts similar to the organ or piano doublings sometimes used as a crutch for normally *a cappella* performance. (One unmistakable example is Mahler's call for trombones and strings to support the entry of a chorus in the Finale of his Second Symphony "only when necessary, to prevent the chorus from dropping in pitch.") But often, by virtue of their tone-color or orchestral placement, such parts throw light on the lines they double or add to the interest of a fully developed orchestral texture that embodies a virtual persona of its own. In concerted vocal-orchestral works, as in solo song, the implicit musical persona speaks on two levels: indirectly through the vocal personas, and directly through the instrumental. The musical, dramatic, and psychological relations between voices and instruments are similar to those obtaining in accompanied solo song.

The case is not always clear-cut. It is sometimes difficult to determine the extent of orchestral independence, and there are interesting borderline examples. In Mozart's "Ave verum corpus," the strings (and organ) essentially double the vocal parts, yet they are more active than the voices, surrounding them with an introduction, interlude, and finale, and occasionally elaborating their melodic lines. Here we have an analogue of the "simple" accompaniment of solo song, in this case accompanying a multiple persona. Insufficiently independent to embody a persona of its own, it is heard as an amplification of the chorus. Evidence in favor of this interpretation is the fact that the hymn is occasionally sung *a cappella*. In this form it still makes perfect sense; it is still heard as the same composition, although diminished in size and incomplete.

One could also play "Ave verum" as an instrumental piece simply by omitting the voice parts. But such is the primacy we naturally accord the vocal persona that we do not accept a performance from which it has been banished as entirely authentic. Even though every note of the instrumental version would be Mozart's own, even though it would be more nearly complete than the purely vocal version, we should tend to consider it a transcription: the work of some arranger who made the decision to suppress the vocal parts. As our habit of indicating their authorship by hyphenating two names implies, we consider transcriptions as hybrids, not as the exclusive expression of the original composer's voice. They are comparable to translations: they offer a similar range of possibilities—and they are similarly unreliable.

A faithful transcription, such as Brahms's left-hand piano version of the Bach Chaconne, subordinates the transcriber's voice to the composer's. Indeed, in transcriptions made for purely practical purposes (like four-hand versions of symphonies), the transcriber's voice is negligible; the performers and their audience (if any) try their best to infer the original from the transcription. (Strictly speaking, every time we perform a harpsichord work on the piano we are playing a transcription of this type!) At the other extreme is Busoni's complete reworking of the same Chaconne, in which Busoni speaks through Bach, rather than Bach through Busoni. At both extremes and in between, exhibiting every degree of variation, are Liszt's innumerable arrangements, paraphrases, and fantasies. Some of these faithfully report the original composer's message; in others one hears above all the voice of Liszt; still others embody a clearly hybrid persona.

The particular type of transcription that interests us here is exemplified by the instrumental performance of the Mozart chorus, for the specific problems raised by instrumental versions of vocal originals elucidate some basic differences between vocal and instrumental music. How are such voice-to-instrument transcriptions to be heard?

Let us approach the problem in a roundabout way. Suppose that we are listening to a familiar song performed in such a way that we cannot make out the text. Perhaps it is vocalized rather than articulated, or perhaps it is translated into a strange language. Although we do not hear the words we know, we can still follow them mentally, rehearsing them as we hear the song. But now suppose that the song is an unfamiliar one, so that we cannot follow the words at all. The presence of the singer nevertheless forces us to recognize the existence of the vocal persona, even though this persona remains, under the circumstances, inarticulate for us. The persona may, in fact, actually *be* inarticulate; perhaps the song consists of nonsense syllables, or pure vocalization (like Debussy's "Sirènes"). No matter: in every case the singing voice invests its melodic line with human personality. We cannot help interpreting the vocalizer, not as the player of a wordless instrument, but as a protagonist who has deliberately chosen to remain inarticulate. We attribute to his song the connotations of words, no doubt on the tacit assumption that although his thoughts are not verbally expressed, they nevertheless could be, and at any point might be.

If we try, we can often listen to transcriptions in much the same way. If the song is a familiar one, its melody is presumably clear to us, and we can mentally follow the text along with it, thus recreating an imaginary vocal persona. We sometimes listen in this way to instrumentally realized cantus firmi, or to strictly instrumental compositions derived from vocal originals, as chorale-preludes are. If the song is not a familiar one, or if we do not remember its words, we can still imagine the melody as representing a protagonist—one who, like the vocalizer, has chosen to remain inarticulate. This is especially easy if the melody is assigned to a solo instrument that can preserve the cantabile character of the line. Indeed, the fact that we refer to lines in general as voices suggests that some such idea influences our perception of all melodies, including those of instrumental origin.

At the same time, the absence of the human voice crucially alters the content of the composition. Only our deliberate effort supplies the melody with words. Only our imagination turns the instrumental line into a singing voice that wishes to remain wordless. If we are willing to let the words go, if we can forget the singing voice, we listen in a different way, and what we hear is different. The experiment as outlined here is hard to make, but it is often possible in the reverse direction. Most of us were familiar with Liszt's "Sonnets of Petrarch" as piano pieces before we realized that they were originally songs—not to speak of his familiar "Liebestraum" No. 3!) When we listen to a transcription as a purely instrumental composition, all that is left of the vocal persona is its melody. Its leading role should, of course, still be distinguishable, but it will have lost its unique position, for any instrumental line may claim, at one time or another, status as a "voice." What is more, the originally vocal melody, once it is separated from voice and words, no longer belongs to the subconscious of a protagonist: he is not there! The line has become what I shall be calling, in the discussion of instrumental music, a *virtual agent*. It is now a component of the instrumental persona, a verbally unspecified subconscious that unites the agent with all the other instrumental parts. The song has become a tone poem, producing its effect through abstract musical means.

According to this view, the human voice occupies a special position among musical instruments. As human beings, we recognize the voice as belonging to one of us, and we accord it special attention. A violin or a clarinet, despite its singing powers, can be dominated, hidden, or superseded by other instruments. It is possible to treat the voice in this fashion, but the result is that it almost inevitably sounds abused. For when the human voice sings, it demands to be heard, and when it is heard it demands recognition. Contrast, for example, the baroque concerto with the aria which it resembles in design. The solo in a violin concerto, say, emerges from the orchestra, blends with the orchestra, disappears into the orchestra. Its priority is intermittent; its leadership is always subject to question. In an aria the voice is always clearly demarcated. One knows exactly when it enters and when it stops. When it sings, it is clearly supreme. The fact that only the human voice can adequately embody a protagonist or character is due to this natural supremacy, more than to its ability to verbalize. For, as we have seen, words are not necessary so long as the voice is there.

This point of view is beautifully supported by a composition that may seem an exception to some of the principles enunciated above: Milton Babbitt's *Philomel*. The dramatic situation requires the soprano to take shape from her electronic surroundings, gradually turning her vocalization into articulate language as the protagonist she portrays, transformed into a nightingale, discovers her new voice. This is a voice in the process of finding itself, but once it has succeeded, there is no question as to its supremacy. So far as I know, this is the unique example of a composition that seems to create its own protagonist, who in turn creates her own song. As such it appropriately symbolizes the relationship between the vocal persona and the musical persona that envelops and includes it—between the protagonist's voice and the composer's.

5

A Lesson from Berlioz

To what extent can the concepts developed to explain the dramatistic structure of the accompanied song be broadened in order to cover purely instrumental music? In the foregoing discussion, it proved helpful to divide the all-embracing musical persona into vocal and instrumental components, but what if there is no vocal persona? Must we stop with the simple assertion that the musical persona is entirely virtual, that is, instrumental, or can we fruitfully subdivide the virtual persona? Specifically, might it not be illuminating to consider each instrument as playing a quasi-dramatic role? A piano, for example, could represent the *persona* of a solo sonata, the *protagonist* of a concerto, and one of the participating *characters* of a trio—granted that each of these must be recognized as only virtual in light of the analogical derivation of these concepts from those found applicable in a more literal sense to the voice.

At least one composer seems to have believed something of the sort. So far as I know, Berlioz never tried to expound a general dramatistic theory of instrumentation, but his treatise on the subject attests on almost every page his faith in the power and the duty of each instrument to individualize and bring to life the musical ideas assigned to it.

Here are just a few examples culled from his pages devoted to the woodwinds: "The feelings of being abandoned, forgotten, and mournfully isolated that this forsaken melody [at the end of the third movement of the *Fantastic Symphony*] arouses in the hearts of some of its hearers would not have one quarter of their effect if it were assigned to any instrument but the English horn."[1] "The lower register [of the clarinet] is well suited, especially in sustained tones, to those *coldly threatening* effects, those dark accents of *motionless rage*, whose discovery is due to Weber's ingenuity."[2] "[The middle and higher registers of the flute] can be used for various kinds of melodies and accents, without however being able to match either the naive cheerfulness of the oboe or the noble tenderness of the clarinet."[3]

It is little wonder that Berlioz's absorbing concern for the expressive character *of* the instruments should lead him to the concept of instrument *as* character—and that is exactly what happened. Here, for instance, is what he has to say about the use of the clarinet in its middle register: "Its voice is that of heroic love; and if the united brasses in grand military symphonies arouse us to thoughts of a troop of warriors clad in glittering armor, marching to glory or death, the sound of numerous clarinets in unison, heard in the same context, seems to represent their women: their beloved wives, their proud-eyed, deeply passionate lovers, who are inspired by the sound of arms, who sing in the midst of battle, who crown the victors or die with the vanquished."[4]

Today we are inclined to laugh at such instrumental personification as a typical excess of ingenuous Romanticism. It may therefore come as a surprise to find Stravinsky adopting a not dissimilar point of view, and in the very book that claims that "music is, by its very nature, essentially powerless to *ex-*

[1] Hector Berlioz, *Grand traité d'instrumentation et d'orchestration modernes* (Paris: Schonenberger [1843]), p. 124.

[2] Ibid., p. 137.

[3] Ibid., p. 154. But read further in this passage to discover what Berlioz considers the true expressive powers of the flute, as exemplified in the famous melody from Gluck's *Orfeo*.

[4] Ibid., p. 138.

press anything at all."[5] In describing a lost *Chant Funèbre* that he had written to the memory of Rimsky-Korsakov, he states that "all the solo instruments of the orchestra filed past the tomb of the master in succession, each laying down its own melody as its wreath against a deep background of tremolo murmurings simulating the vibrations of bass voices singing in chorus."[6] Nor is this his only remark of the kind.

The practical results of Berlioz's dramatistic approach can be observed in the *Fantastic Symphony* and *Harold in Italy*. Despite their programs (expressly stated in the one case, implied in the other), the techniques they reveal have interesting applications to absolute music as well. Indeed, precisely because, like transcriptions, they contain a "silent" verbal component, they may help us shift our discussion from the vocal to the instrumental medium. So, before turning to the specific question of instrumentation, let us look briefly into Berlioz's attitude toward these "silent" words.

The only explicit program that Berlioz ever wrote is that of the *Fantastic Symphony*. There are two distinct versions.[7] In the earlier, the first three movements present "various situations in the life of an artist," and the last two, a dream induced by an overdose of opium. In the later version, the dream embraces the entire symphony. This modification emphasizes the fact that Berlioz's intent, even in the first instance, was not to describe scenes and incidents, but to depict his hero's reactions to them.[8] More than this, the transfer of the entire action

---

[5] Igor Stravinsky, *Stravinsky: An Autobiography* (New York: Simon and Schuster, 1936), p. 83.

[6] Ibid., p. 37.

[7] For the texts of both versions, together with a comparative discussion of the two, see my edition of the symphony in the Norton Critical Scores series (New York: 1971), pp. 18–35.

[8] Berlioz makes this clear in a footnote to one of the early editions of the program, where he firmly rejects, for example, the "notion of painting *mountains*"

to the dream world may have been an indication of the composer's realization—subconscious, no doubt!—that the mental experiences informing his music were primarily those of the subconscious.

Berlioz's position, then, seems to be that an instrumental composition is the communication of an experience, transformed into abstract sound. A program can tell us something about the subject of that experience and the specific circumstances giving rise to it. But the experience the music records is not the event described by the program; it is the reaction of the subject to that event, a reaction that may be largely or entirely subconscious. What I call the complete persona of instrumental music is this experiencing subject.

Programs vary greatly as to the exactitude with which they identify the persona. Berlioz's lovelorn artist is a character whom we feel we know, and whose experiences we share. The figure behind *Les Préludes* is much less clearly individualized: he is Everyman, passing symbolically through the stages of life. The experiencing subject implied by *La Mer* is unspecified; he is characterized only by his reactions to varying aspects of the sea.

One principle is clear: the persona is always to be distinguished from the composer. We must recall here the difference between the John Keats who tells us of hearing the nightingale and the John Keats who wrote the poem. The same distinction applies to program music. Even if we decide that the subject experiencing "cheerful feelings on arrival in the country" is a character named Ludwig van Beethoven, this Beethoven is not the composer. He is an artistic construct—a self-portrait, as it were—through whose reactions Beethoven the composer con-

---

in favor of the attempt to express "*the emotion* aroused in the soul . . . by the sight of these imposing masses."

veys his message to us. Similarly, neither the embattled hero of *Ein Heldenleben* nor the paterfamilias of the *Sinfonia Domestica* is identical with the man who composed both works. Strauss seems to have grasped this principle imperfectly, if at all. Instead of taking advantage of the relative objectivity afforded by its exploitation, he devoted a great deal of energy to a fruitless endeavor to make us accept his own self-evaluation: to convince us, in musical terms, of his devotion to his artistic ideals and of his deep affection for his family. As a result, both works are marred by passages that are ludicrous for their bombast or their sentimentality.

Berlioz was wiser. The program of the *Fantastic Symphony* is, in its own way, just as autobiographical as those of the Strauss works, as the composer freely admitted in letters to his friend Humbert Ferrand. He wrote of a new symphony "in which the development of my hellish passion is to be portrayed";[9] later he referred to it as "my novel, or rather my story, whose hero you will easily be able to recognize."[10] Nevertheless, the hero is not Hector Berlioz but "a young musician." (So he is called in the programs; the sequel to the symphony christens him Lélio.) In choosing as his persona a figure *identifiable as* Berlioz but not *identical with* Berlioz, the composer was symbolizing—no doubt unconsciously, but nonetheless appropriately—the relationship of every composer to his musical voice. The persona's experiences are not the composer's experiences but an imaginative transformation of them; the reactions, emotions, and states of mind suggested by the music are those of the persona, not the composer.

The role of the young musician as the single experiencing subject of the *Fantastic Symphony* is clarified and strengthened

[9] Hector Berlioz, *Lettres intimes* (Paris: Calmann Lévy, 1882), p. 64. Letter of Feb. 6, 1830.
[10] Ibid., p. 66. Letter of April 16, 1830.

in the second program, which envisages the entire work as a representation of his opium dream. According to the first program, the earlier movements might mistakenly be construed as attempts at objective narration of the hero's actions and states of mind; they might seem to present the hero as observed rather than the hero as observer. This would be especially true of the second and third movements, with their elements of literal description. The new program forbids us to think of the symphony in this way, for it insists that all is in the mind of the hero. The ballroom, the landscape, the piping shepherds, the thunder—what is significant is not that these are elements of a dream, but that they are all subjectively experienced. Only through the subject can we know them at all. Music, Berlioz is saying, can never hope to depict the external world of objects and events, nor should it even try to do so. Its field is the inner life of the experiencing subject. Thus, if the persona of the young musician symbolizes the composer's voice, the dream in the second program is no less than a symbol of musical content itself.

A musical composition, then, according to Berlioz, records and communicates an inner personal experience, and this is as true of a symphony as of a solo. Yet at the same time, within the complex orchestral texture of such a work as the *Fantastic Symphony* the instruments often appear to be leading lives of their own—to be speaking, acting, reacting, in quasi-human fashion; and here we return to the dramatistic concept of instrumentation that set us off on our investigation of this composer's views. For, side by side with his faith in the predominance of the musical persona, Berlioz exhibits a belief in the personality of the musical instrument. Almost more than any other composer he can convince us, not just that instruments *have* personality, but that instruments *are* personalities.

One must be careful here. It is not the material instrument that is personified, but the energy it transforms—kinetic into sonic—and transmits. Thus our discussion properly refers to the *sound* or *voice* of an instrument rather than to the instrument itself. But even Berlioz is not always precise in his usage, for the more correct locution would soon prove tiresome. Since the shorter version is clear enough as long as it is recognized as a convenient abbreviation, I have not hesitated to employ it.

Berlioz's complete musical persona—a *virtual orchestral persona* in this case—is thus a composite. Like the complete persona of an accompanied song, which was implied by the interaction of voice and accompaniment, this one too is an implicit persona, to be inferred from the interrelationships of its component instrumental personalities. (When the orchestra accompanies one or more voices, then the composite orchestral persona in turn becomes a component of a still more complex whole.) If we wish to think of the persona as a narrator, the instruments are characters in its story. Or if the persona is dreaming, the instruments people its dreams. The persona is in control; yet the instruments appear to move of their own free will.

Probably the most obvious example of instrumental characterization in the *Fantastic Symphony* occurs in the "Scene in the Country," where the oboe and the English horn represent two shepherds in friendly dialogue. This much we know from the program, but the meaning is made clear by compositional devices as well: the placing of the oboe offstage; the quasi-recitative style; the antiphonal and imitative texture; the nature of the accompaniment, subdued where it is not absent altogether; above all, the return of the English horn at the end of the movement, waiting in vain for the oboe to answer its phrases. One should note, too, how Berlioz has reserved his instruments for this occasion. The English horn appears nowhere else in the symphony. Even the oboe color has been unusually restricted in the preceding movements, appearing in pure form only in one episode and in the coda of the first movement (mm. 360, 456, 493 ff.). And throughout the third movement, after the introductory dialogue, the pure oboe color is restricted to two brief passages in which it echoes other instruments, just as it does in the introduction (mm. 67, 153–154). It is clear that the English horn and the oboe, although voiceless, assume roles as virtual characters, or, as I shall call them in order to distinguish them from actual characters, *virtual agents*. Like the characters in an opera, they must obey the formal demands of the music; but, again like operatic characters, they must appear to move freely—to compose their own parts, as it were. Here, too, the conductor is the surrogate of the composer's persona: That is, by directing the performance, he symbolizes both the composer's actual authority over the musical events and the persona's imaginary control. At the same time he must recognize the virtual agents' needs to express their own individuality. He is successful when he achieves the difficult balance between the requirements of the musical design and the instrumental agents' urge to freedom.

Unlike real characters, however, instrumental agents move on a purely musical, nonverbal plane, and they communicate solely by what I have called symbolic gestures; hence the division between the verbal-conscious and the vocal-subconscious components of the vocal psyche does not apply to them. Therefore we attribute to the agent what we deny to the character: full awareness of its musical nature and musical environment; indeed, that is all an agent can be "conscious" of, for it exists only in its musical context. Pursuing the vocal-subconscious analogy, one might say that the agent "thinks" only on the subconscious level—that the subconscious is the locus of its consciousness. (Thus we do not consider it dramatically inappropriate for instrumentalists, who personify virtual agents, to act overtly aware of one another, or for a soloist to enter into a personal engagement, as it were, with the rest of the orchestra.)

Agents are by no means limited to leading roles; indeed, as we shall see, every orchestral instrument, at all times, either is or contributes to the formation of an agent. But only when a single instrument is individualized—when, for the duration of a movement, a theme, a measure, or only a short motif, it is clearly characterized in some way—does it become, like the oboe or the English horn of the "Scene in the Country," what I call a full-fledged *unitary virtual agent*. If such a unitary agent maintains its role fairly consistently throughout a movement or an entire work—as the solo of a concerto notably does (or, in another context, any member of a chamber ensemble)—it is a *permanent agent*. But in the course of a complex orchestral work most instruments perform shifting functions. Only from time to time will one achieve the rank of unitary agent. Berlioz often signals the emergence of such a *temporary agent*—especially when it might otherwise be overlooked—by the direction "solo." As he uses the term, it is not always to be understood in the normal orchestral sense of designating a leading solo part or melody. Instead it may indicate that the player should give special attention to a part that, although not necessarily predominant, has graduated from mere membership in the group to a more favored rank—that of temporary unitary agent.

The magical horn entries toward the end of the introductory Largo of the *Fantastic Symphony* (mm. 50 and 54) are marked in this way, and it is easy to see why they should be so designated: the horns clearly represent unitary agents here. But what of the first and second violins during the same passage? They are assigned characteristic counter-melodies in a layout obviously suggestive of a dialogue. Solo instruments performing these lines would certainly be recognized as temporary agents; accordingly, each violin section merits similar status. Although we cannot call it a unitary agent, each section as a whole assumes the function of a virtual agent to be inferred from its unanimity of action and expression. Let us therefore call such a group an *implicit virtual agent*, as distinct from the more explicit unitary agent.

It is not feasible, even in a symphony by Berlioz, for all instruments always to realize what Elliott Carter calls their "built-in 'character-structures,' so to speak, which can be suggestive of musical possibilities both on the level of sonority and on that of actual musical behavior." [11] Nor is it necessarily desirable. It is interesting and illuminating to find that Berlioz foregoes strict individualization when he introduces the most famous "character" in his symphony, the Beloved herself. Why does he assign her theme, the *idée fixe*, not to a solo instrument but to a combination of flute and violins? There are, I think, two reasons, one programmatic and one purely musical. In the first program, the Beloved never actually appears in the first movement—indeed, it is not clear whether she appears anywhere in the story, except in the fevered brain of the artist. In contrast to the real shepherds of the "Scene in the Country," she takes part in the opening movement only as an imagined character. At moments, however, particularly at the ends of movements, the Beloved's image seems to become clear to the hero, taking on a hallucinatory reality. At these points her theme is assigned to solo instruments—especially, as the symphony progresses, to the clarinets. (A solo clarinet depicts her, for example, at the end of the waltz and at the moment of execution. These partial statements of the theme, by the dulcet A-clarinet and the harsher C-clarinet respectively, prepare for its parody in the "Witches' Sabbath." There it is assigned first to the C-clarinet when the Beloved appears in the distance, and

[11] Allen Edwards, *Flawed Words and Stubborn Sounds: A Conversation with Elliott Carter* (New York: Norton, 1971), p. 67.

to the squeaking E♭-clarinet when she arrives on the scene; it is soon doubled by other instruments as she is welcomed by the crowd.)

The musical reason for the nonsoloistic exposition of the theme is probably the more basic. The theme is not just the representation of the idea of the Beloved; it is the first subject of a sonata exposition. Hence it should not be heard simply, or even primarily, as a characteristic melody. Its line is a source of motivic material; its accompaniment provides harmonic and rhythmic connections with much that follows; even its tone-color is a subject for future development. Under these circumstances, the kind of expression called for by a unitary agent might well prove misleading. The theme is therefore stated by an implicit agent—one again implied by the unanimity of an instrumental group, this time a combination involving a mixture of tone-colors.

Berlioz called the *idée fixe* of the *Fantastic Symphony* a double one, for he thought of it as comprising both the melody and the "beloved image" it was intended to portray. The *idée fixe* of *Harold in Italy* is also double, but in a different way: it is both a theme and an instrument, a permanent unitary agent— the solo viola. Although the symphony is supplied with no program beyond the titles of the movements and occasional comments within them, it is almost certain that both melody and instrument represent aspects of the hero, another alter ego of the composer in the guise of Byron's Childe Harold, so perhaps we should call the *idée fixe* a triple one, since it embraces theme, instrument, and character. The theme, after an orchestral adumbration, is stated by the viola; thereafter it remains the viola's peculiar, but by no means exclusive, property. The problem of the overpersonalization of a sonata subject is avoided here, for the viola theme is announced in the introduction, not in the exposition proper. It does enter the sonata-allegro and each of the succeeding movements in turn, sometimes stated by the viola, sometimes not; but it is always an observer, so to speak, rather than an actual participant in the form of the movement.

This twofold method of musical representation enables Berlioz to unify his symphony with a flexibility unknown to the *Fantastic*. The viola is not restricted to the theme, the theme is not restricted to the viola: the two enter into varied relationships with each other and with the other elements of the movements in which they take part. If the viola represents Childe Harold himself, the theme is probably intended to emphasize one facet of his nature, for example, his melancholy introspectiveness. But it is neither fruitful to speculate on the specific meaning of the theme nor possible to decide it. What is significant is the general principle illustrated here. The viola, like any other agent, can entertain many ideas, of which the Harold theme is one. The theme, like any other musical motif, can be repeated by one instrument after another, with or without variation, as if expressing the same idea occurring to each of several agents in turn. The analogical correlation between instrument and character is thus matched by that between musical idea and mental idea. Once more the program of the *Fantastic Symphony* furnishes a suggestive comparison. The original version explains the double *idée fixe* as follows: "The beloved image never appears before the mind's eye of the artist without being attached to a musical thought." Broadening this correspondence to fit any context, programmatic or nonprogrammatic, we might say that every musical gesture conveys an idea or image in the minds of the agent making the gesture and of the musical persona.

It is interesting to contrast what we might figuratively call Berlioz's "autobiographical technique" in the two symphonies. In the *Fantastic*, the artist-hero, although never to be confused with the actual composer, nevertheless stands very close to him, for the artist can be identified with the musical persona of the symphony. In the later work, the distance between the composer and his representative, Harold, is much greater. The latter is not the persona of his symphony; he is a character in its implied program—the chief one, the hero if you will, but still only a character; and he is confirmed as such by being assigned one theme (among many) and one instrument (among many). Yet the symphony must not be considered as an attempt at objective narration, for, if I have interpreted Berlioz correctly, every composition reports a subjective experience. Who, then, experiences this symphony? Is it Harold himself, reviewing the scenes of his youth at some later period, or is it yet another surrogate of the composer, an unnamed persona? The music cannot tell us, nor has Berlioz revealed his intention in words. It is enough for us to realize that the programmatic technique here reveals a greater detachment of the composer from his subject, who is now treated as "he" rather than as "I." It should thus be no surprise that the composer's next symphony, *Romeo and Juliet*, eschews autobiography entirely, devoting itself instead to the exposition of a well-known literary theme, in part by frankly dramatic methods.

Harold in Italy, then, reflects the experience of an unspecified musical persona. What keeps it in the programmatic category is the fact that it is possible to fasten identifying labels on some of its virtual agents and their thematic ideas. But it is by no means necessary to do so, for the labels of a program have no intrinsic connection with the musical elements to which they are attached. Despite possible correspondences between music and program through imitative devices, coincidence of formal pattern, and agreement of general expressive character, any specific verbal formulation is bound to be largely arbitrary. Berlioz was aware of this, as he showed with respect to the *Fantastic*

Symphony when he used for the "March to the Scaffold" a movement originally designed for another context (the "March of the Guards" in *Les Francs-Juges*), and when he altered his original program. Moreover, his eventual permission to perform the symphony without distribution of the program implied that, however useful it might have been to him in forming and organizing his musical images, and however suggestive to the original audiences trying to understand his novel expressive intentions, it could nevertheless be dispensed with once it had done its job.

The concepts of persona, agent, and idea, on the other hand, are basic—and not to the comprehension of program music alone. Freed of the burden of verbal associations, they are applicable to absolute music as well. For that matter, absolute music can be defined as music in which persona, agent, and idea are verbally unspecified—and, it is important to add, unidentifiable.

It should be possible, then, to generalize the categories used to analyze Berlioz's approach to program music so as to throw light on all instrumental music. For any instrumental composition, like the instrumental component of a song, can be interpreted as the symbolic utterance of a virtual persona. This utterance may be a symbolic play, in which a number of virtual agents assume leading roles. It may be a symbolic monologue, in which a single agent addresses an audience. It may be a symbolic soliloquy, a private utterance that an audience overhears. Very likely it is a complex structure involving all these modes, which parallel the three voices Eliot found in poetry. But in every case there is a musical persona that is the experiencing subject of the entire composition, in whose thought the play, or narrative, or reverie, takes place—whose inner life the music communicates by means of symbolic gesture.

In broadening the concept of virtual agent to cover all

instrumental music, I must interpret it in a less restricted way than the above examples might imply; for I have in mind something less specific than Carter does when he speaks of the sense of instrumental personality developed during the classical period: "The sonorous characteristics and behavioral possibilities of the instruments play a role not only in that they suggest varied and distinct kinds of musical materials, but also in that they become dramatic identities that can be played off against each other in many ways and thus actually help create the musical argument itself."[12] For Carter, as, I suspect, for Berlioz, instrument *as* character depends on instrumental character. Hence Carter finds this dramatic element lacking, for example, in the relatively uniform instrumentation of the baroque. I interpret the Second Brandenburg Concerto, say, in which trumpet, oboe, violin, and flute state the same fugue subject in turn, as involving no less role playing or personalization than a Berlioz symphony or a Carter quartet. The drama is of a different kind—reasoned discussion and mutual emulation, perhaps, rather than emphatic self-expression—but it is drama nevertheless.

We have already seen how the unison of several instruments can imply the existence of a single virtual agent. The possibility of such implication, however, is not limited to this technique. Melodic doublings of all kinds, chords of uniform color, blocks of blended sound—all these can be media for the embodiment of implicit agents. Indeed, an implicit agent can be any recognizably continuous or distinctively articulated component of the texture: a line, a succession of chords, an ostinato, a pervasive timbre. It is an important part of the conductor's job to decide at every point whether a given instrument should be considered an individual or a member of such a group. As a member the instrument must inevitably sacrifice much of its freedom,

12 Ibid., p. 68.

but the implicit agent assumes a character of its own, analogous to that of a unitary agent.

Many instrumental components, although identifiable as unitary or implicit agents, are relegated to positions in the background of the musical texture, where they function as accompaniment. Under such conditions it would obviously be inappropriate for them to express their instrumental personalities obtrusively, but that does not mean that they must lack character. Indeed, one test of well-written music is the extent to which accompanying agents, while clearly subordinate, are individualized.

Agents, then, can be permanent or temporary, unitary or implicit, leading or subordinate. And every instrumental composition can be described in terms of the interaction of all its agents. Whether the work is for orchestra or for chamber group, for ensemble or for solo, intelligent performance demands that its agents and their functions be clearly distinguished.

What makes a unitary virtual agent of an instrument is its assumption of a specific role in a musical context. It is not the exploitation of its technical idiosyncrasies that turns it into a metaphorical character, but its individualization as the maker of a significant musical gesture. One obvious kind of personalization is invoked every time we refer to an instrument as "singing," and to its melody as a "voice," but this is not the only kind. A piano, which can simulate many voices; a bass drum, which can simulate none: these are no less open to personalization than the normally monophonic clarinet or horn.

As we have seen, the role playing of the unitary agent may be permanent, lasting throughout a given work; this is the case with the viola of Harold, or with the solo of a concerto. On the analogy of vocal protagonists, one might call obviously leading parts of this kind *virtual protagonists*; and indeed, the terminology is suggestively relevant to one way (although not the only way) of listening to a solo concerto. Chamber music, too, depends on permanent characterization, although it is rarely desirable or even possible to single out any instrument as the protagonist.

Orchestral music, on the other hand, abounds in temporary agents. Some examples have already been cited from the *Fantastic Symphony*. Two more will serve to illustrate contrasting techniques by which such temporary personalization can be made effective. The recapitulation of the first movement of Beethoven's Fifth Symphony contains a famous oboe cadenza that fills in what, in the exposition, was a fermata on the dominant. Here is a perfect example of the gradual assumption of a role. A comparison of the exposition and the recapitulation of the opening theme reveals that the woodwinds play a much more striking part in the latter; here flutes, first oboe, clarinets, and bassoons all contribute to the harmonic background of the theme, in contrast to the exposition, in which only the bassoons are heard, doubling the cellos. It is from this new woodwind background that the oboe gradually detaches itself, assuming a melodic independence that flowers in the little cadenza. After its moment of glory, it returns to the background, again joined by its colleagues. Here, then, is a melodic line—a "voice"—that individualizes an instrument that has been almost constantly present but never in the foreground.

In contrast, a well-known movement by Tchaikovsky presents the extraordinary instance of a virtual agent created by the simplest possible gesture: a single sound, heard once only during the course of an entire symphony. Lacking obvious preparation and follow-up, its very isolation is a significant aspect, so to speak, of its personality. I refer, of course, to the famous gong stroke in the Finale of the Sixth Symphony. Technically, the effect is one of extreme simplicity. But once we begin to think of the gong in dramatistic terms, its role becomes bafflingly mysterious. Was it always "there," waiting for us? Or was it engendered by the climax of the movement? Does it remain behind us as the movement continues? Or does it disappear once the energy of its single stroke is dissipated? (The hammer blows in Mahler's Sixth Symphony raise similar problems, together with an additional one: why was the third blow eliminated?) Questions like these can never be answered definitively, but every responsible performance must somehow come to terms with them.

At the opposite extreme from temporary characterization is the role of the pure solo instrument. The violin of a Bach partita, the piano of a Beethoven sonata—the agents these bring to life are coterminous with the musical personas of their respective compositions. Unlike the persona of an orchestral or chamber work, implicitly emerging from the collaboration of a number of agents, the virtual persona of a solo composition is unitary—identical with a single unitary agent. This union of virtual agent and musical persona is far closer than the corresponding relationship between vocal and musical persona in simple song, which is the nearest analogue in vocal music to an instrumental solo. There, it will be remembered, only the implicit musical persona can normally be construed as fully aware of both words and music. But the instrumental agent is imagined as existing precisely through its musical thought, and when, in a solo work, that thought is the complete composition, unitary agent and complete persona coalesce into one unitary virtual persona.

Often a single instrument—whether a solo or a member of a group—is responsible for a number of melodic lines or other musical components. In this case, the unitary agent's part, like that of a complex instrumental persona, embraces a number of subsidiary roles. Each of these can be construed as implying its own agent. Unlike the implicit agents defined earlier, which were inferred from the unification of a number of individuals, these are inferred from the subdivision of a single individual's part. The performer on a keyboard instrument, especially, is responsible for many implied roles. An important part of his job is to decide just what, in every passage of a composition, constitutes such an implicit agent. This category should not be narrowly interpreted as including only leading components. Every note of the piece, like every instrument of the orchestra, must help define some agent, permanent or temporary. Whether to "bring out an inner voice," whether to play a passage as a melody with accompaniment or as a series of chordal blocks, whether to isolate accents or to incorporate them in a more inclusive line, sometimes even whether to play with one hand or two—all these decisions depend on an interpretation of the dramatistic structure of a piece, on an apprehension of the extent and nature of the role of each implicit agent, as much as on formal criteria narrowly defined. Or perhaps form, from one point of view, consists in the establishment and the precise definition of these roles.

A few examples may indicate how certain interpretive problems can be clarified by considerations of this kind. Why does the first movement of Beethoven's *Sonata quasi una Fantasia* Op. 27 No. 2 seem intolerably sentimental if the melody is made unduly prominent in performance? Is it not because a temporary implicit agent has been mistakenly converted into one that, by its insistence, seems permanent? Imagine the same movement transcribed for violin and piano. The violin, whether it is playing or not, is always "there"—a permanent agent. When it is silent it is resting, waiting for its next cue. The sentimental performance applies this kind of interpretation to the implicit agent of the melody. But this does violence to Beethoven's conception, according to which the melody is a temporary agent, arising out of the accompaniment and at times sinking

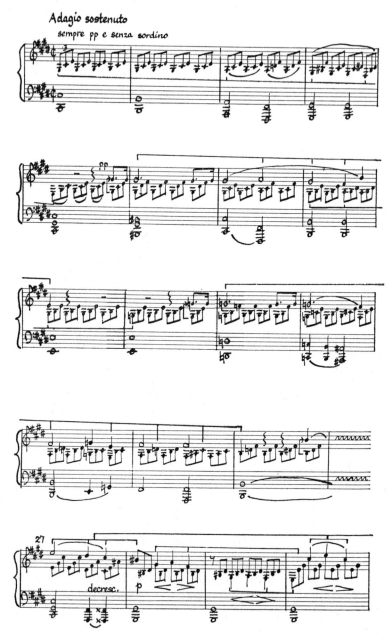

7. Beethoven, *Sonata quasi una fantasia* Op. 27, No. 2, first movement. The connecting beams suggest the way important melodic lines move from accompaniment to leading part and back again. Note especially in mm. 27–33 how the melody gradually dissolves into the accompanying arpeggios, and in mm. 40–46 how it emerges through the successive augmentations of the motif stated in triplet eighths at the beginning of m. 40.

back into it (Ex. 7). When it disappears for the last time, its motif is echoed by an inner voice, which at this point emerges to assume a temporarily individualized role. The plasticity of these relationships is vitiated if the melody—by transcription or by unbalanced projection—is allowed excessive predominance.

In contrast, Chopin's Nocturne in D-flat Op. 27 No. 2 can be fairly successfully transcribed. Its melody assumes the dominating role of a protagonist. Hence, when it is enriched by parallel thirds and sixths, the effect is not that of the entrance of a new agent, but rather of a pianistic simulation of the added opulence of double-stops on a violin.

But a succession of parallel intervals on the piano does not always imply a single agent. In Schumann's Romance in F-sharp Op. 28 No. 2 parallel thirds are consistently divided between the two hands; moreover, they are embedded in an accompaniment figure characterized by a contrary motion that emphasizes the independence of each hand—an independence confirmed by later developments in the piece. Thus the thirds are best taken as standing for not one but two agents, although some unanimity between the two is indicated by the parallelism and supported by the title.

Multiple stops on a solo violin, for that matter, are not necessarily to be construed as contributing to the elaboration of a single agent. Contrapuntal part writing, as in many movements by Bach, usually suggests two or more implicit roles. An especially interesting passage, where subsidiary agents implied in this manner assume full instrumental individuality, is found in Stravinsky's Violin Concerto. At one point in the last movement the solo violin embarks on several measures of two-part counterpoint, naturally rendered by double-stops (rehearsal no. 116). Here the polyphonic writing clearly implies two agents, and as if in fulfillment of this implication, another solo violin (drawn from the orchestra) takes over one of the melodic lines (no. 117). The new agent's job is finished when the coda begins, *subito più mosso,* so it vanishes—ostensibly into the original solo part, actually into the violin section of which it is a member. An understanding of the way this role emerges, as if graduating from the imagination of the protagonist to achieve independent existence, is essential to its intelligent performance.

There are no rules to determine just which components and combinations should be considered as implying virtual agents; the decision in every case must be made according to the musical context. Sometimes, particularly in chamber music, the requirements of an implied role (for example, a melodic line) come into conflict with the demands of an individual agent for recognition. The resulting tension is often a source of great musical interest. To see a few of the ways that Beethoven exploits this tension in his late quartets, look, in Op. 130, at the end of the Alla danza tedesca, and at the interplay between the two violins in the Cavatina; in Op. 131, at the theme of the variations, and at the pizzicato transition that leads into the recapitulations of the Scherzo; in Op. 133, at the sections marked "Allegro molto e con brio." In each of these cases the principal melodic line moves from one instrument to another, temporarily creating what might be called a *simulated virtual agent,* an effect necessarily at odds with the permanent instrumental characterization. A development of the same technique underlies twentieth-century *Klangfarbenmelodie.*

The tension between melodic line and instrumental individuality is also involved—less overtly, but no less surely—in orchestral doubling and sectional reinforcement. When a line is assigned to a string section, or to several wind instruments, or to any other unison or octave combination, we almost automatically assume what I have hitherto implied: that a completely uniform effect is intended. Actually, in every case we should ask to what extent each member is to be considered as a dramatic individual, and to what extent a mere component of an implicit agent. More frequently than we might expect, something akin to the multiple persona of the chorus functions in orchestral music. A multiple agent of this kind, rather than the implication of an individual agent, may often be what Berlioz has in mind when he puzzlingly designates an entire string section as "soli." The pizzicato contrabass interjections that underline the pauses in the opening theme of the Largo of the *Fantastic Symphony* (mm. 12 and 14) might profit from such an interpretation, which could lead to a livelier performance than one based on the assumption that a single agent is implied. And certainly the humor of the trio section in the third movement of Beethoven's Fifth Symphony depends on the effect of a number of contrabasses and cellos scrambling to keep their part in the fugato up to tempo. (Contrast this passage with the recitative for the same instruments at the beginning of the Finale of the Ninth Symphony. Here they evidently imply a single virtual agent—since it is to be transformed, in fact, into a single actual character.)

More complex doublings sometimes suggest that we are meant to be acutely aware that more than one kind of instrument is playing a single melody. The extraordinary octave combination of solo violin, oboe, and horn that Brahms introduces in the recapitulation of the Andante of his First Symphony (mm. 90–98) has been criticized for failure to blend; but doesn't the subsequent independence of both the horn and the violin indicate that the composer wants us to be aware of their individuality all along?

In general, however, the use of doubled and multiple parts tends toward implication of roles. Lines so performed are bound to be less personal to the individual performer, but by the same token they can appear to express the complete musical persona more directly. Instrumental music expresses the complete persona more immediately than song, which communicates primarily through the vocal protagonist; in the same way music largely dependent on implied roles expresses the complete persona more immediately than music in which individual instruments retain the status of unitary agents. It is no accident that the nineteenth century saw the rise both of the symphony orchestra and of the solo piano, for both impose a style of composition rich in the implication of roles. In each, a single figure —the pianist or the conductor—represents the persona directly and visibly.

It is thus important to preserve in performance the solo or ensemble character of every component. To assign the Third Brandenburg Concerto to a body of symphonic strings, to transcribe the *Grosse Fuge* for string orchestra, to subject the winds of a classical symphony to indiscriminate doubling—such practices basically alter the expressive meaning of the music. The work thus produced may be a good one, but it is a new work. Compare, for example, Webern's Five Movements for String Quartet Op. 5 with his arrangement of the same work for string orchestra. In the latter, delicacy of individual characterization is necessarily sacrificed in favor of overall sweep and pervasive atmosphere.

In considering the relationships between instrumental agents and the players who bring them to life, one must never forget that the agents are, after all, only virtual. They are not embodied by their performers as vocal personas are. The singer *enacts* a role, *portrays* a character. The instrumental performer, too, is in part an actor, but one that *symbolically personifies* the agent of which his instrument in turn is but the concrete vehicle—for, once more, the instrument as sound, not as object, is the locus of the agent.

It follows that a player, unlike a singer, is rarely to be thought of as composing his part. As I put it before, in connection with the instrumental accompaniment of song, the music should give the effect of composing itself *through* the player. This phrase can now be expanded: the effect of composing itself through the player by means of an instrument. In a chamber work, for example, each agent is to be conceived as composing—experiencing, living through—its part under the guidance of the implicit persona, the central intelligence in whose mind all the agents subsist as components. What the performer does is parallel, but by no means identical. His task—as mind, that is, not as muscle—is to *think through* his own part in relation to all the others, and to the whole. Because of this close parallelism he becomes a symbolic personification of the agent.

I might just as well have said: the music should give the effect of composing itself through the instrument, by means of the player. For once the relationship of performer, instrument, and agent has been clearly established, it is unnecessary—indeed, hardly possible—to make a hard and fast distinction between performer and instrument. Whether one thinks of the performer as the motive power of his instrument, or of the instrument as an extension of the performer, for musical purposes they are almost as indissoluble as a singer and his voice. This is, in fact, the way we tend to think of a good performance: as the achievement, not of a musician or of an instrument, but of a compound creature, the musician-*cum*-instrument.

If good performance is inspired and controlled by the concept of the complete persona, it is no less an awakening of that persona. An instrumental persona, like its component agents, is actualized only through instrumental sound. Sounds are not a means of mediation by which we are enabled to hear music; they constitute the reality of music, and they effect the realization of its persona. The persona of a composition for a single instrument is *symbolized* by the musician-*cum*-instrument, but it is *realized* in the voice of that instrument. The persona of a violin partita is a violinistic persona; the persona of a piano sonata is a pianistic persona. And the persona implied by a combination of instruments is realized in the sound of the combination.

The voice of an instrument is not to be narrowly construed as an abstract or ideal sound; it is the actual sound as conveyed through the mechanics of an instrument by the energy and dexterity of a player, and its character depends on the potentialities and limitations thus defined. Instrumental technique, that is to say, determines the nature of the persona to the extent that it defines the possibilities available to it. The positive content of instrumental virtuosity is to be understood in these terms. If we interpret a passage like the end of the second movement of Schumann's Fantasy Op. 17 as the pianist's struggle against the limitations of his instrument, we are endowing the composition with a spurious human protagonist to be portrayed by the musician. If we think of the performance as an extraordinary achievement of muscular coordination, we turn the performance into an athletic event. But if we regard the coda as the gesture of a pianistic persona that adopts extreme methods in order to express extreme attitudes, pushing musician-*cum*-instrument to unprecedented efforts, the virtuosity required for its realization becomes a symbol of the strenuous musical content. In contrast, music in which the effort required is not matched by a corresponding content does produce an empty display of pure athleticism.

There is a supposed category of abstract compositions, conceived for no specific instrument or instrumental combination, and even supposed to deny the necessity for such material aids to realization. *The Art of Fugue* is sometimes held to typify an ideal music of this kind, for which mere physical sound is only an approximate exemplification. Now, it may be possible in the realm of Platonic Ideas to conceive of sounds that possess pitch but lack color; nevertheless, it is difficult for a mundane intelligence to understand how. If *The Art of Fugue* is to be apprehended as music, even in the imagination of a gifted score reader, it must be heard or thought of as a series of tones. Tones, whether real or imaginary, are necessarily associated with wave forms, and wave forms produce the effect of timbre. Thus, even if *The Art of Fugue* were indifferent to instrumental realization, that would not mean that the work could dispense with such realization. It would imply rather that the formal and expressive values the music incorporates are not closely associated with any specific instrumental characteristics and are hence to a certain extent independent of them. Actually, recent scholarship strongly supports the theory that the entire *Art of Fugue* was designed as a keyboard work.[13] If this view is correct, then the nature of the persona, if not uniquely designated (harpsichord, organ?), is nevertheless clearly defined in instrumental terms.

If we wish to find compositions that obviously permit a variety of realizations we should look in the literature of the sixteenth century—at Giovanni Gabrieli's canzonas, for example. Yet even here the choice of instrumentation is not unlimited. The musical values of, say, the first of his *Canzoni per sonar a quattro* ("La Spiritata") would hardly be preserved in an arrangement for vibraphone, ukulele, chimes, and contrabass—or, it might be added, in a version along the lines of Webern's idiosyncratic transcription of the six-part ricercar from *The Musical Offering*. For the style of any music tells us a good deal about the virtual agents required to project the characteristics of its persona. Thus our canzona suggests a performance by four instrumental voices, all capable of sustaining lively and

[13] See, for example, Heinrich Husmann, "Die 'Kunst der Fuge' als Klavierwerk," *Bach-Jahrbuch* 35 (1938), 1–61.

emphatic melodic lines, mutually balanced in dynamics, and probably not greatly differentiated in tone-color. A setting that observes these limits will allow the persona to speak; one that violates them will inhibit it.

The canzona could be performed, then, by a brass quartet—to mention one group that meets the persona's requirements. But it could also be played by a full brass choir, or by a string orchestra, or by a single organ. We accept it as the same composition, regardless of whether it is performed by one instrument, or four, or many, because we recognize that its form depends on the interplay not of instruments but of instrumental voices. These can be assigned equally well to unitary agents or to agents implied by string sections or by keyboard lines. Gabrieli's persona in this case might be considered as indeterminate, since it does not call for a specific set of virtual agents; but it is not abstract. Its musical thought must still be communicated through instrumental sound, actual or imagined.

In sum, the concept of the complete musical persona must be as multifarious as that of musical composition itself. The persona may be unitary, as in a piano solo; or it may be implied, as by a group of instruments. It may combine verbal and musical components, as in song; or it may be entirely virtual, as in instrumental music. It may be well defined or relatively indeterminate. It is to be posited as an intelligence embracing and controlling all the elements of musical thought that comprise a work. These elements subsist in its consciousness, which is in turn awakened by the performance (in actuality or in imagination) of the gestures that express them.

Look once more at our readings of "Erlkönig," from yet another point of view. If the five voices of *d* suggest the component strands of a complex composition, then let *a* stand for the unification of them all under the control of the complete persona. And as the poetic persona expresses itself through the narrative-dramatic line of the entire poem, so the musical persona is implied, not by any single component or progression, but by the interaction of all of them, by the comprehensive line of the whole. Above all, the persona is realized in the total rhythmic life of the composition, for the composite rhythm, more than any other musical element, controls the interrelationships of all motifs and progressions.

Sometimes the complete persona is summed up and visually represented by a single figure: the piano soloist, the conductor. Sometimes, as in a concerto or a song, there is a protagonist whose point of view offers us a mediated approach to a comprehension of the full persona. Sometimes, however, as in chamber music, the persona can only be inferred from the interaction of equal agents. The instruments, so to speak, evoke a subtle but discernible presence through their communication with one another—a communication for which the proper metaphor often ought to be "thinking together" rather than "talking together." That is why at a good chamber recital one frequently has the feeling that one is overhearing the players, who in turn symbolize the persona communing with itself. Here, certainly, we find examples of Eliot's private poetic voice as applied to musical composition. (An intimate solo performance can sometimes produce the same effect.)

Tape-recorded electronic music goes even further than chamber music in its lack of a single, easily comprehensible analogue of an often subtle and complex rhythmic structure, for it dispenses with the visual component altogether. Sometimes it is said that electronic music dispenses with the performer; sometimes, that it depends on a single ideal performance by the composer himself. But if it does, what we hear is not the performance; that was completed with the preparation of the master tape. What we hear is a reproduction, a recorded instance of that performance. The effect is not of the composer performing the music, but of the music performing itself. Hence there is wisdom in David Lewin's remark: "It is ... improper to say that a composer 'performs' his own electronic piece; rather he executes it, as a painter executes a painting."[14]

Agents, both unitary and implicit, may seem from time to time to take part in the progress of an electronic piece, but they are simulations: no instruments or performers are really there. The electronic persona is unitary, and it is uniquely embedded in and embodied by a single performance (or execution) of its music—a characteristic that it shares, amusingly enough, with the pieces Haydn and Mozart wrote for mechanical organs. (It may also be one that it shares with recorded performances of conventional compositions. When we listen to a recording what we hear is not a performance but the recorded instance of one. We should never forget this, even though we may not be prepared to admit that recorded "voices" and "instruments" are not real voices and instruments, but simulations.)

Some contemporary music—electronic or conventional—is so kaleidoscopic in timbre and pointillistic in texture that a dramatistic analysis would be hard put to find in it more than a rapidly shifting series of temporary agents, simulated or real. In this case it might be preferable to dispense with the concept of agent altogether and to hear the piece only in terms of the complete persona, which must marshal all elements, no matter how disparate, into some kind of comprehensible pattern if the music is to make sense. In music of this kind, certain tone-colors and textures may function as ideas rather than characterize agents. (I find it illuminating to listen to portions of Stravinsky's *Movements* and *Variations Aldous Huxley in memoriam* with the latter possibility in mind.)

Another extreme is exemplified by those avant-garde works

[14] David Lewin, "Is It Music?", *Proceedings of the First Annual Conference of the American Society of University Composers* (1966), 50–51.

in which the histrionic element is so strong that the instrumentalists have become full-fledged play actors. For in these productions, which are properly speaking dramatico-musical rather than musical, they no longer symbolize virtual agents but portray characters. True, as characters they may be called upon to play their instruments; their real job, however, is not the playing but the impersonation. For as characters they are likely to have to do a number of things besides simply playing: to improvise, to record their own performances, to play against recordings of their own performances, to use their instruments for unusual purposes, and to do things completely unrelated to their musical abilities. Whether an implicit musical persona can take shape at all under such circumstances is doubtful.

Much contemporary music, however—even much electronic music—still depends on the joint continuity of line and timbre that I have discussed in terms of virtual personalization. This locution may seem only a more colorful way of talking about musical progression; even so, its use may demonstrate that in music, as in any art, formal and expressive concepts are not separable but represent two ways of understanding the same phenomena. For the sense of progression that animates persona and agent, and allows us to follow their fortunes, is the same sense of progression that underlies our comprehension of musical form.

At the same time, we must not forget that music consists of motif as well as progression, and dramatistic analysis may prove especially helpful in clarifying relationships between musical motifs and the larger forms to which they contribute. I have suggested that a motif is a gesture conveying an idea or image in the "mind" of an agent. But the idea is equally in the mind of the complete persona, as everything in the composition must be. In song, the situation may be more complex still, for a musical idea may often be taken as representing the subconscious component of a vocal character's thought, even when that idea is instrumentally voiced. Such motifs may thus have a triple significance—for the character, for the instrumental agent, and for the complete musical persona. This is especially true of Wagnerian leitmotifs, which, contrary to common opinion, seldom represent persons or objects—except when they imitate sounds like Siegfried's horn. Usually a leitmotif corresponds to a character's unspoken attitude toward himself, another character, an object, or a situation. It presents a mental, not a physical image. Often the clearer such an image becomes —the closer a character comes to a conscious realization of its full import—the firmer its instrumental characterization becomes. Note, for example, how the "gold" motif—which, by this account, represents not so much the Rhinegold itself as its effect on others—moves from the tentative dominant of the horns to the definitive tonic of the trumpet as the treasure gradually reveals itself to the Rhinemaidens and Alberich (and to the audience) in the opening scene of *Das Rheingold*. The motif belongs, as it were, to the trumpet, and it is always announced by the trumpet when its significance is to be most immediately and vividly appreciated.

The investigation of the relationships between musical agents and the ideas they entertain often suggests a kind of "abstract program." In fact, it is usually a pattern of this kind, derived by analogy from a verbal program, that constitutes the musically relevant aspect of the latter. But the same kind of abstract program can be found underlying absolute compositions as well. Thus, in the traditional analysis of fugue, the use of the terms "subject," "answer," "exposition," "discussion," and "summary," suggests the model of a conversation on an announced topic. Among sonata-related forms, the solo concerto especially cries out for dramatic interpretation, for it displays attitudes on the part of the protagonist and the orchestra that vary from mutual support to downright opposition. In particular, a work such as Berg's Violin Concerto, with its obvious personal references, cannot be intelligently followed without a tacit reliance on concepts that make its dramatistic structure comprehensible. Only within such a framework can one make sense of a musical design that juxtaposes original contemporary materials with quotations from the traditional literature of folk song and chorale. If one thinks of the solo violin as a virtual protagonist, one can imagine it as *listening* to the orchestra: developing the tone-row from hints thrown out by the other instruments; being reminded of the "Kärntner Volksweise" by the brasses; sharing with the woodwinds the evocation of "Es ist genug." It is not necessary, and not even advisable, to try to identify the respective roles here—as an individual and his environment, say, or as a young girl facing Life and Death. For a musician the roles "solo violin" and "orchestral instruments" are sufficiently clear, and they are much richer in suggestion than any specific programmatic interpretations. But I insist that they are *roles*. They are not mere elements of design, transformed into sound by human energy applied to mechanical contrivances; they are imaginary intelligences expressing themselves in the symbolic gestures of sound through the aid of sympathetic musicians-*cum*-instruments. The thoughts and attitudes they convey and the experiences they undergo are basically human, for in the last analysis all roles are aspects of one controlling persona, which is in turn the projection of one creative human consciousness—that of the composer.

6

Participation and Identification

Works of art that require realization in performance properly occupy an ill-defined area between ritual and game. All of them are basically dramatic, and their dramatic nature can come to full expression only when they successfully resist the temptation to occupy either extreme. True, ritual and drama probably had a common origin, but an important distinction has developed between them. Drama depends on the pretense that its characters are actually living through their portrayed experiences—ostensibly for the first and only time. Ritual, by contrast, is the frank repetition of a received liturgy; its efficacy as ritual depends on its being openly recognized and accepted as such a repetition. And at the other pole, games are forms of recreational activity whose course and outcome cannot be predicted, even (and especially) by the participants.

Today—as perhaps long ago—the tensions between these positions are often resolved in favor of the extremes. Some avant-garde theatrical productions seem to require their actors to assume the roles of celebrants rather than of characters, to recite prescribed formulas rather than to imitate actions. Other productions encourage improvised freedom to the extent that the actors (and often members of the audience as well) give the effect of participating in a rather poorly organized sports event.

Similar tendencies toward either ritual or game are discernible in certain musical manifestations today, most notably in theatrically staged multi-mixed-media presentations, or happenings, or what you will, that involve music, or sounds that, for want of a better word, are called music. But in the long run these cannot pose a serious threat to what some of us, at least, consider the more basic musical values of technical control, intelligible structure, and intrinsic expression. Much more dangerous, I am convinced, is the subtle and pervasive influence of a special kind of ritualism, one that inappropriately transforms many of our musical performances into liturgical services and that encourages our audiences to respond to them accordingly.

I do not mean what is sometimes called the ritual of concert going, although no doubt that, too, has its unfortunate effects. What I mean is an attitude all too common nowadays among musical connoisseurs. Our more knowledgeable audiences tend to regard a composition as a received text. Even if it is not played as one, it is heard as one. The performance is taken by the cognoscenti, not as a lived experience, but as the reverent reading of a sacred writing. Or, in less figurative language: the ideal performance is assumed to be no more and no less than the accurate and convincing presentation of a precomposed text. Of course the ideal performance *is* the accurate and convincing presentation of a precomposed text, but to hear it only as such is to deny music its expressive power.

Part of the blame for this situation rests, no doubt, on the severely restricted repertoires of most of our opera houses and concert organizations: it is hard to make overfamiliar compositions yield vital experiences. We have followed every Beethoven symphony every step of the way so often that we can no longer summon up any excitement or suspense in response to one more repetition. We have exhausted them as compositions—ironically enough, without ever really getting to know them, for the exhaustion is usually the result of a surfeit of superficial hearings. True, we still listen, but no longer to the music. We hear only performances of an abstraction called The Score, performances that we constantly measure against one another or against a hypothetical ideal. As a result, we do not really experience even the performances: we criticize them—failing to realize the futility of all criticism that is not based on vivid experience of both performance and composition.

Recordings, too, encourage the attitude that what one is hearing is religiously fixed—in this case, the reading as well as the text. As a result it is not uncommon to find a standard recording accepted by many as *the* composition, from which all other interpretations are considered to some extent deviant.

This unhealthy state of affairs reflects the fact that our contemporary musical culture is more interested in the preservation of the past than in the development of the present. But only a culture that takes a lively and genuine interest in the art of its own day can preserve the art of its past in more than ritualistic fashion. This principle works in the other direction as well, for a ritualistic attitude toward the art of the past inevitably results in a similar attitude toward all art, and hence toward the art of the present. And so we find "advanced" audiences today receiving the latest music in the same spirit of religious acceptance that they consider appropriate to the masterpieces of the past. Here is music that, whether it attracts or repels them, should excite them; it should be, in a word, an experience. It is often nothing of the kind. Instead, it has become a ritual.

What is almost worse, this attitude has infected musician as well as auditor, and the performer of new music as well as of old. Interpretation, like the arts it serves, recognizes the extremes of ritual (slavish literalness) and game (idiosyncratic freedom). By all accounts, the spirit of the game seems to have overcome many of the virtuosos of the late nineteenth century; at any event, the spirit of ritual rules today. Instead of asking himself, "Am I experiencing this music and conveying my experience to the audience?" the musician asks, all too often, only, "Am I playing this correctly? Am I following the rules of observance?" (He adopts this attitude even toward those contemporary pieces designed as "games" rather than as "compositions," transforming the possibly amusing game into a solemn rite.) In part, this point of view reflects an admirable desire, nourished by modern historical scholarship, to present the composition in a form as close as possible to its composer's original conception. But it also signifies a refusal to accept the further obligation to revitalize the composition as a dramatic gesture and thus to recreate it as the living experience that must have been basic to that conception.

In accepting the ritual repetition of a sacred text as their model for musical performance, both the musician and his auditor reject the possibility of *identification* with the musical persona or with any of its components. But just this sense of identification underlies all valid performance and all intelligent listening. I mean nothing mystical or mysterious by the word. What I have in mind is an active participation in the life of the music by following its progress, attentively and imaginatively, through the course of one's own thoughts, and by adapting the tempo and direction of one's own psychic energies to the tempo and direction of the music.

The members of Bach's congregation who sang the chorale melodies in unison with the choir during the performance of his cantatas were participating in this way, even though they were no doubt prompted more by religious than by esthetic motives. Schumann approached the same kind of identification from a purely musical point of view when he wrote of Berlioz: "Of course his melodies are not to be heard with the ears alone; they will pass uncomprehended by those who do not know how to sing along with them inwardly—not in an undertone, but with full voice. Then they will take on a meaning that seems to grow in profundity the more often they are repeated."[1] Schumann is encouraging the listener to participate in the musical performance by identifying himself with the virtual agent of its melody and by following that melody through the simultaneous creation of a parallel version in his own mind. In so doing, the listener narrows the distance between instrumental agent and vocal character. By inwardly singing, he promotes the agent to what we might call a potential character, personified through the medium of an imaginary human voice.

The promotion is, of course, unnecessary in vocal music, and the ease with which the listener can indulge in participatory identification—which, to be complete, should involve words as well as music—may be one reason for the popularity of song and opera with untutored audiences. But I suspect that identification here is often facilitated less by the unique prominence of the melody than by the commanding position of the soloist, or by the sympathetic nature of the character portrayed. Instead of legitimately identifying himself with the vocal persona by mentally enacting a parallel version of its artistic role, the listener may, in common parlance, "identify with" the singer or the character—a form of participation that takes his attention away from the music. He is especially likely to find the object of such identification in the personality of a singer of his own sex and age, and he will try to participate in the life of the vocal protagonist by investing it with the charms of that personality. In his eyes, or ears, the singer becomes the character, and he can "identify with" both—a daydream particularly inviting to young or naive listeners.

A similar ingenuousness often underlies the untutored response to instrumental solos as well, to concertos—to any per-

---

[1] From his essay on the *Fantastic Symphony*. Robert Schumann, *Gesammelte Schriften über Musik und Musiker*, 5th edition, Martin Kreisig, ed. (Leipzig: Breitkopf und Härtel, 1914), Vol. I, p. 80.

formance that presents a clearly commanding figure. The most obvious example is the conductor of a symphony orchestra. As we shall see, the visually kinetic aspects of these performers can be of legitimate help to the listener trying to make contact with the musical persona. But such a performer, especially if he is a star, runs the risk of tempting his auditors to participate in his exciting activity through identification, not with the music, but with his glamorous personality.

Another highly personal form of participation in vocal music consists of the listener's identification with the supposed addressee of a song. A love song, especially when sentimentally interpreted by an attractive singer, might elicit such a response from an impressionable auditor of the opposite sex. A woman, for example, listening to a tenor singing the "Ständchen" from *Schwanengesang*, might imagine herself as the object of the protagonist's affections and declarations. She would then be converting the simulated rhetoric of Schubert's song into the actual rhetoric of a true serenade, turning a work of art into its functional model. To be sure, even a purely functional serenade would prove a very inefficient means of wooing if its recipient were not in some measure open to the effects of its musical expressiveness—that is, if she were not at least subconsciously participating in its musical line. On the other hand, the serenade would fail of its effect if the lady's attention to the music supplanted her awareness of her own position as an object of suit. Conversely, a simulated serenade fails as a work of art whenever a listener's identification with its imagined recipient takes precedence over conscious participation in the music itself.

The relation just described between the lieder singer and his auditor is hypothetical, but the reactions of female audiences to crooners in the past and to present-day pop vocalists are not. These reactions result from an unfortunate conjoining of both types of overpersonal reaction: the members of the audience identify the singer with the vocal protagonist, and themselves with his addressee. What they are basically enjoying —if that word is appropriate to denote the hysteria that often overcomes them—is not the music but their own imaginary roles (roles that some fans apparently try to act out in real life).

There is no precise analogue to this kind of identification in the response to instrumental music—although I suppose that the ladies who swooned before Liszt liked to imagine that he was playing directly to and for them. (The same belief is encouraged by peripatetic restaurant violinists.) There is, however, a kinship between the auditor who engages in imaginary role playing while listening to a singer and the one who enjoys instrumental music as a background for his daydreams. Both are using the music as a means to self-indulgent fantasy; neither is really listening to it. If they receive its message at all, they do so unconsciously.

Schumann would have rejected all such intensely personal reactions as irrelevant. He would have insisted that although significant participation in music is bound to be subjective, the listener must nevertheless achieve it within the music itself, by following and inwardly reproducing its melodies and progressions. Nor can one stop with such partial identification. In some of his "Musikalische Haus- und Lebensregeln," maxims written for the edification of young students, Schumann points toward an ideal of musicianship that should inspire the listener as well: "You must not learn your pieces with your fingers alone; you must be able to hum them to yourself without using the piano. Sharpen your power of imagination to the point that you can keep in mind not only the melody of a composition but also the harmonies that belong to it."[2] And again, "What does it mean to be *musical?* You are not musical when you play through your piece painfully, with your eyes anxiously fixed on the notes; nor

[2] Ibid., Vol. II, p. 164.

when you get stuck and cannot go on—because someone has turned a couple of pages for you at once. But you are when you can almost guess what is coming in a new piece, when you have memorized a familiar piece—in a word, when you have music not in your fingers alone, but also in your head and heart."[3] The goal of participation must be identification with the complete musical persona by making its utterance one's own. This, I believe, is what Roger Sessions has in mind when he explains "musical understanding": "Understanding of music, as relevant for the listener, means the ability to receive its full message. . . . In the primary sense, the listener's real and ultimate response to music consists not in merely hearing it, but in inwardly reproducing it, and his understanding of music consists in the ability to do this in his imagination."[4] Hindemith makes the same point: "While listening to the musical structure, as it unfolds before his ears, [the hearer] is mentally constructing parallel to it and simultaneously with it a mirror image."[5]

Despite the goal of complete identification, we should not think of Schumann's inward singer as merely representing a stage in one's musical development that one can outgrow, or a stage in one's appreciation of a given composition. Even though one may identify oneself ultimately with the entire persona, that identification necessarily depends on imaginative participation in the musical life of each of its chief components—just as in reading a novel, to understand the author's point of view one may have to enter the minds of all its principal characters. It is impossible to arrive at the complete identification by going *around*, rather than *through*, the partial: one cannot really know a fugue if one cannot trace the individual voices.

[3] Ibid., Vol. II, pp. 167–168.

[4] Roger Sessions, *The Musical Experience of Composer, Performer, Listener* (Princeton: Princeton University Press, 1950), p. 97.

[5] Paul Hindemith, A *Composer's World* (Cambridge: Harvard University Press, 1952), p. 16.

In particular, recognition of a musical protagonist and participation in his fortunes is essential to the comprehension of any composition in which such a character or agent plays the leading part. It may seem obvious that one should grant the primacy of a vocal protagonist and try to arrive at a full appreciation of his role as the leading component of the complete persona. Nevertheless, one can sometimes be deceived by the prominence of an instrumental agent, as in the tenor chorale stanza of Bach's Cantata No. 140 (*Wachet auf*), where the elaborate string obbligato might be taken as primary, at the expense of the chorale melody. (The same misreading might especially infect a performance of the chorale-prelude derived from the movement.) The voice is inevitably the most fully human element in any musical texture in which it takes part. Although an ideally complete identification must include the instrumental roles as well, the participating listener should be able to experience these primarily—although by no means exclusively, and not always finally—from the point of view of the voice. It is Wagner's own failure to appreciate the importance of this principle that produces the discomfort many of us feel at the end of *Tristan*. Wagner himself must have assumed the orchestral persona as primary here, no doubt because of its recapitulatory function. The result is that the listener, after trying in vain to come to terms with the vocal line, often ends by considering it as musically superfluous and turning his primary, if not his exclusive, attention to the orchestra.

The solo concerto is the obvious instrumental form in which recognition of the protagonist and sympathy for his point of view are prerequisite to a synoptic understanding of the composition. It is recognition of the protagonist that inclines one to hear a work as a concerto and not as a symphony. Through sympathy for his point of view one can arrive at an appreciation of the precise nature of his relationship with the orchestra. Is the solo a member of the orchestra, growing out of it as in Bach's concertos? Is the orchestra primarily the accompaniment of a virtuoso, as in many nineteenth-century examples? Do solo and orchestra engage in a dramatic dialogue, as in the later concertos of Beethoven? Could the soloist reasonably conduct the orchestra as well as play (Mozart), or would that be a violation of his role (Brahms)? All these questions are getting at what might be regarded, not too fancifully, as the protagonist's attitude toward the orchestra. Clearly the answers are crucial to an adequate conception of the concerto, a conception that depends to a large degree on thinking through the entire work from the protagonist's point of view. It is this dependence, indeed, that identifies the protagonist as such, regardless of whether the work is actually called a concerto; it is what distinguishes a true protagonist from an incidental solo part. We have already found one obvious candidate for a true instrumental protagonist in a work called a symphony, *Harold in Italy*; it is equally obvious that one does not have to consider the entire *Fantastic Symphony*, or even the entire third movement, from the point of view of the English horn.

At the same time, one should never restrict one's point of view to that of the solo; the risk of a gravely one-sided conception of the work would be even greater than when the protagonist enjoys the clear primacy of the human voice. Thus—except perhaps when the orchestra is relegated to a position of background neutrality—every situation must be considered equally with regard to its effect on the orchestra, which, one must assume, adopts a certain attitude toward the solo. During the opening ritornello of Beethoven's Third Concerto, not only is the piano waiting for its moment to enter, but the orchestra is determining that moment. At the beginning of his Fourth, the orchestra listens to the piano and then comments on what it has heard, and the piano is conscious of being so attended. That is what distinguishes the one from a symphony, the other from a piano sonata, even at the outset. (The visual aspects of performance are certainly helpful in making such attitudes obvious; perhaps they are even necessary. And why not? The physical conditions entailed by the performance of a work are an essential constituent of its expressive content. Recordings and broadcasts thus depend to a large extent on the hearer's ability and willingness to infer these conditions from prior knowledge and from audible cues.)

The final view of the concerto is the synoptic one. It should now be clear, however, that this view, which is that of the complete musical persona, cannot dispense with the partial attitudes of solo and orchestra. It can never totally replace them; on the other hand, it cannot merely combine them. It must synthesize them. One who achieves full identification with the complete persona of any complex work must not only participate in the fortunes of each component persona, character, and leading agent, but also experience, vividly and intimately, the course of events produced by their relationships.

Above all, to achieve identification a listener must fully comprehend the composite rhythm that constitutes the locus of musical form, and he must synchronize his own psychic movements with the symbolic gestures audibly embodying that rhythm. Perhaps eighteenth-century audiences, because of their presumable familiarity with the actual steps of the dances that so often defined the movements of suite and sonata, sometimes found it easier to arrive at complete identification by following rhythmic patterns rather than melodies. Be that as it may, this approach is certainly valid and useful. Suitably adapted, it may prove fruitful when applied to relatively amelodic compositions of today. Nevertheless, no matter which path is traversed, the goal of complete identification should be the same. To hear a composition in this way is, no doubt, an infrequently realized ideal; yet it is an ideal that must implicitly inspire any attempt to comprehend a composition as something more than pure design on the one hand or an opportunity for emotional indulgence on the other.

The concept of imaginative participation and the consequent levels of identification apply to the performer with perhaps even more immediate relevance than to the listener. The performer may find that an appropriate sense of identification not only enables him to solve the problems created by the tension inherent in his activity, but even forces them to contribute significantly to the vitality of his performance. For, as we know, every performer, instrumental as well as vocal, is in part an actor, and as an actor he leads a double existence, on the actual level of his own personality and on the dramatic or symbolic level of his role. Like a good actor, he must exploit the resultant tension creatively, by freshly interpreting the role in the light of his own personality. If he is successful, it must be because he has in some way identified personality with role. For the singer, this means the fusion of person with persona already suggested as his goal; identification is thus available to him as a dramatic actuality. But an analogous condition must be achieved by instrumentalists as well. Such identification will operate on the level of symbolic personification instead of true impersonation, although it should be no less vividly experienced.

This principle can be seen at work in the musical parallel of a common theatrical situation. An actor, as a person, can never be surprised by any event in a play; obviously, he knows everything that is going to happen ahead of time. But the character must often be surprised, and on such occasions it is the job of the actor to portray this surprise. Now, I maintain that a good actor somehow, on some level of his psyche, really *is* surprised, even though he knows in advance that he is going to be surprised. In the same way, a musician knows—we hope—

everything that is going to occur in a composition; therefore he can never be surprised by anything that happens. Yet on occasions he is confronted by a deceptive cadence, say, or a sudden fortissimo chord. If, in the context of the piece, these are meant to be startling events, he must convince his audience that they are indeed startling, and he can do this only if he succeeds in being startled himself. (Yes, even the players of Haydn's "Surprise" Symphony must somehow surprise themselves; otherwise they will never jolt the audience.)

In one sense, the effect I have been describing is an illusion: the performer cannot *really* be surprised. But in another sense it is not an illusion. The good musician immerses himself so completely in the flow of the music that, for the duration of the performance, his own experience becomes identical with the course of the music. As an actual person, thinking about the composition, he can relate every passage to its past and to its future; he knows all that has happened, is happening, and will happen. But in his symbolic role he identifies himself with the musical persona, or with his own component of that persona, so completely that he lives through its experiences, as if for the first time. To be sure, his knowledge of the entire composition still functions, even on this symbolic level; that is what makes his performance unified and consistent. But at every point, his knowledge of past events becomes memory; knowledge of the future, foreboding. His synoptic overview of the entire composition is translated into an immediate experience of each event in its order of occurrence; this is what brings his performance to life.

The ideal performance of instrumental music thus involves the same paradox that characterizes vocal performance: it is simultaneously predetermined by the composer and under the control of the performer(s). The extent to which the one or the other factor predominates varies according to personal

and stylistic requirements. For some musicians, complete identification seems possible only if they remake their roles in their
own images; others are capable of adapting their personalities
to those imposed by the music. Historical styles, too, differ in
their attitudes toward freedom of interpretation. The improvised embellishments and variations expected of eighteenth-
century soloists, when judiciously added to elaborate the composer's basic musical or musico-dramatic conception and not to
display the performer's technique, were no doubt of great advantage in establishing the latter's identification with his role.
The illusion that each performance presented an experience as
lived through rather than rehearsed could be supported by the
addition of fresh details; insofar as this occurred the performance was actually, as well as fictively, a new experience. At the
same time, the fundamental outlines of the musical structure,
representing the composer's persona and symbolizing his authority, remained clear. In the nineteenth century this kind of
collaboration fell out of favor, except in old-fashioned hold-
overs like the coloratura of an Italian aria or the cadenza of a
concerto; even here the practice of writing out such passages in
full eventually supplanted the earlier usage. During this period
virtuosos became "interpreters," perhaps because they were de-
nied the more overt opportunities of collaboration. From this
point of view, "interpretation" is a laudable attempt to ensure
the vitality of each performance—again by making it actually,
as well as fictively, a fresh experience. When it goes too far it
ends in exaggerated mannerism, but at its best it supplies a
healthy spontaneity to readings that might otherwise become
ritualistically literal.

Carter must have this sense of spontaneity in mind when
he says: "From a purely musical point of view, I've always had
the impression of improvisation of the most rewarding kind
when good performers take the trouble to play music that is

carefully written out as if they were 'thinking it up' themselves while they played it—that is, when with much thought and practice they come to feel the carefully written-out piece as a part of themselves and of their own experience, which they are communicating to others directly from themselves in the moment of the performance, in an alive way."[6] My own formulation puts it somewhat differently. The effect should not be that the player is improvising the music, but that the music is composing itself through the combined agency of player and instrument. Yet this result can be obtained only under the conditions of identification of player with role that Carter has so well described.

There is, to be sure, an art of pure improvisation, in which the paradoxical tension between freedom and predetermination is resolved in favor of complete liberty on the part of the performer-composer. An exhilarating sense of excitement often results, but it is usually gained at the expense of important formal values. On the other hand, music that depends on recorded media for its realization, as much electronic music does, resolves the tension in favor of the opposite pole. In music of this kind, the formal control can embrace every detail to an extent impossible in conventional media; but by the same token, sufficient repetition of music so realized produces in the listener a sense of knowing in advance just what is going to happen. It is ironic that real jazz, which celebrates improvisatory freedom, should be permanently available to us only through recordings, which freeze every performance into a single, unchangeable version!

True improvisation is often deliberately simulated by music that is in actuality carefully composed; such passages as the introduction to Beethoven's Choral Fantasy Op. 80, or any written-out concerto cadenzas, aim at this effect. Their per-

[6] Allen Edwards, *Flawed Words and Stubborn Sounds: A Conversation with Elliott Carter* (New York: Norton, 1971), p. 78.

former must assume a role analogous to that of the singer of a simulated natural song. Somewhat like the participants in those contemporary works I have called dramatico-musical, he portrays a character, for he is impersonating as well as performing. In this case, however, his portrayal is a basically musical one, for he impersonates a composer-performer who is supposedly improvising the passage in question. Only in the guise of this composer-performer can he participate in the music itself. (In this connection it is interesting to realize that the present introduction to the Choral Fantasy stands for an actual improvisation by Beethoven himself at the premiere.)

A related effect, on a more abstract or symbolic level, is the object of passages like the introduction to the Finale of Beethoven's Sonata Op. 106. Here, I insist, the composer's intention is to convey a sense that the pianistic persona itself, rather than the player, is improvising—searching for the proper musical material from which to construct the succeeding movement. If music is normally to be heard as composing itself, this music is heard at the stage of precomposition. Again, a strong histrionic flavor must permeate its performance, but here the pianist is not portraying a composer-performer in the act of public improvisation; instead he must convey the impression of the persona of the sonata trying to order its own musical thoughts so as to arrive at its final self-realization in the fugue.

It is often loosely said that in such passages we are in the presence of Beethoven at work, wrestling with his musical matter and forcing it into shape. The pianist, then, should try to identify himself with the composer. This view rests, however, on a confusion between composer and persona that obliterates the very distinction that I have been at pains to draw; moreover, it is rendered untenable by Beethoven himself in his evident attitude toward a similar passage, the introduction to the Finale of the Ninth Symphony. Here, too, a period of improvisatory indecision is succeeded by a choice of theme and formal pattern. When this movement from chaos to order appears to fail, the first words uttered are: "O Freunde, nicht diese Töne!" The plural "Freunde" shows that these words are addressed not to the composer but to the orchestra: to the virtual agents that make up the orchestral persona. They, not Beethoven, are held responsible for the course of the music up to that point. Perhaps the extraordinary dissonances that begin and end the orchestral section imply that the orchestra is as yet insufficiently under the control of the complete persona; perhaps the recitative of the lower strings is a representative of that persona, attempting to establish control by calling up one theme after another until the desired end is found; perhaps, finally, the virtual agent of the recitative, aghast at the return of disorder, bursts into human voice, transforming itself into an actual character in an act of self-transcendence. Be that as it may, the unique drama of this passage must be interpreted in some such symbolic way, and not as a representation of the composer's personal struggles.

The analogy between performer and actor can be helpful in analyzing the performer's job on occasions like this, and the similarity between the two extends to situations that are much less overtly histrionic. But the performer must be constantly responsive to demands that go far beyond those normally imposed on the actor. One of the most important of these involves the performer's relations with his fellows.

Now, a good actor must certainly be a good listener; in fact, only because he is a good listener is he a good speaker—because, that is, he listens not only to his own words but to those of every other character as well. The actor who knows only his own part does not know his own part, for each role is defined in large measure by its connections with others.

So much is obvious, and its analogy with musical performance is obvious. The individual player must listen carefully, both to his own part and to those of his colleagues; he must know their parts almost as well as his own; and so on. But every ensemble player is continually confronted by a situation actors rarely if ever have to face: he and his colleagues are performing simultaneously, not in turn. If he is to hear them, he must do so while he is playing as well as when he is silent. (This applies, of course, equally to singers.)

The difficulty here may not seem insuperable: it is after all possible to divide one's attention and to do more than one thing at a time—although it is hard to keep one or more of them from becoming mechanically routine. But the task becomes more problematic when one considers the question of identification. Successful performance depends on the player's identification with his role. But complete comprehension of a composition would require his identification, not with his single role, but with the musical persona as a whole. Except for conductors and pure soloists, then, it would seem that performers are barred from a full appreciation of the music they are playing! Now, we might all agree that the listener is in a better position to grasp the full import of a symphony than, say, the second oboist; but does the listener really understand a violin concerto better than its soloist?

The answer once again depends on the recognition of a state of tension. Every performer must be at the same time a member of his own audience; indeed, he should be the first and foremost member. Qua performer, his primary identification, the only one fully available to him during the performance, is with his own role; qua listener, he relates that role to the entire musical complex, and in so doing participates in the complete musical persona. The resulting tension is not unlike the one we all feel when we face contrasting and sometimes conflicting responsibilities as individuals and as members of a social group. But whereas the personal tension, if acute, often leads to frustration and neurosis, the musical tension is one of the prime sources of creative vitality in performance. It is the exquisite balance of the demands of each individual against those of the group that informs well-played chamber music, making it a delight both to take part in and to hear, and this balance can be achieved only if each player is constantly aware of his double orientation.

The ascendancy of the ideal of the chamber musician over that of the virtuoso elicits the best performances of concertos, too, of songs, even of operas. A warhorse like Tchaikovsky's First Piano Concerto yields unexpected delights when jointly undertaken by a soloist and a conductor who understand and expound the relations between piano and orchestra; a Mozart opera intelligently produced as a vocal-instrumental ensemble is an occasion for public celebration.

It would be wildly utopian to hope that the chamber-music ideal might permeate our symphony orchestras—to imagine that the third bassoon player might study an entire movement in order to understand the significance of his single phrase and to decide accordingly how it should be projected. As it is, most decisions of this kind, if they are made at all, are left to an overburdened conductor; as it is, orchestral players seldom study scores, even of new works; hence, as it is, new works are subjected to inept performances by orchestras that have never taken the time or the trouble to learn them.

The chamber-music ideal applies equally to pure solo performance. When a pianist lavishes so much attention on a melody that he plays the accompaniment in perfunctory fashion, or when he temporarily emphasizes a subordinate voice without clarifying its origin and its destination, he is identifying himself too closely with the component in question, with insufficient consideration for his responsibility to the whole. One sometimes hears a pianist adversely criticized for "playing like a chamber player," by which is meant, I suppose, that he plays in a subdued and colorless manner. Actually the phrase should be a term of high praise, signifying that the pianist understands and projects the interrelationships among all the components that, together, convey the complete persona.

The relation between the various levels of participation and identification can perhaps be clarified by comparing three of a pianist's tasks. Consider in turn the solo pianist, the duo-pianist (one of a two-piano team), and the piano-duettist (one of a team playing four hands at one piano). The soloist can identify himself fully with the complete persona of a composition, for in this case it is identical with the unitary virtual agent of his own part. Its components are at most implicit agents; nevertheless, the pianist must project the individuality of each, relating it both to the other component agents and to the whole. This he can do only if in learning the piece he has bestowed full attention on each component. The partial identifications consciously achieved at that stage all contribute, if only subconsciously, to the complete identification of the performance, which depends on the player's properly balanced participation in the life of every implicit agent.

The duo-pianist's part, too, will comprise implied roles in which the performer must participate, but in this case they go to make up a unitary agent, not the complete persona. At a higher level the duo-pianist participates in the life of the total persona, just as at a lower level he participates in that of his own components. As a listener, he must experience the former as fully as he can; as a performer, he must completely control the latter. But his primary identification is with a virtual agent, the single piano part.

The duettist's position is anomalous. His role, like the duo-pianist's, might seem to be that of a unitary agent, but if it is, it is singularly incomplete. He shares his very instrument, over which he thus loses a measure of control. He may not be pedalling, or he may be using only the soft pedal. The implied agents often move back and forth between him and his partner, for their parts in general seem determined more by convenience of keyboard position than by musical continuity. What all this suggests is that the aim of four-hand music should be to evoke a single persona, not by the interaction of two agents, but by the blending of two players into a single four-handed monster. Each must sacrifice more of his individuality than in a normal ensemble, for four-hand playing is a marriage rather than a mere friendship. Such a performance is thus a peculiarly intimate affair, and when it is undertaken in public, the auditor may feel at best an intruder, at worst a voyeur.

Anomalous though the duettist's position may be, the activity is one that sensitive musicians find deeply satisfying. Since neither four-hand player represents a full-fledged agent, each can identify himself more directly with the complete musical persona than he can in any other form of ensemble performance. Normally, chamber players are colleagues in a mutual enterprise, but the four-hand player feels that his partner is an extension of his own personality, each participating fully and equally in the life of the persona they jointly symbolize. This is why transcriptions of four-hand works for two pianos, even faithful ones like Karl Ulrich Schnabel's version of Schubert's Grand Duo,[7] fail: they substitute two unitary agents for one fused persona. And perhaps this explains why four-hand arrangements of symphonies and the like are so popular: in addition to their convenience, they make it possible for almost anyone to gain the first-hand experience of playing through the score without the necessity of assuming a spurious soloistic or ensemble role. In four-hand music one's job is simply to assume one's share of the total pianistic persona.

[7] (Milan: Edizioni Curci, 1949).

7

Further Paths to Identification

The successful performance of chamber music, which I have held up as a model for the best performance of music in general, depends on familiarity with the entire score on the part of each participant. Short of minute attention to performances repeated impractically often, careful score reading is the only road to this kind of knowledge. (An unhappy corollary, that madrigal singers who sang only from part books never attained this ideal, is probably valid. A four-hand player today can appreciate the problem, from his frustration in trying to visualize a complete score from the comparatively simple part book that, for pianistic convenience, is usually supplied.) Score reading is often described as if it were only a kind of abstract listening. It is not: it is also a kind of abstract performance. It is the only kind of performance of an ensemble work that permits a musician (the reader) to identify himself fully and intimately with the complete persona, and that gives him total control over the direction of the persona's musical activity. This is as true of conductors as of players. A conductor's identification is based on his reading of the score, or on his accurate memory of it, not on the always imperfect and at best approximate realization of his conception by an orchestra or chorus over which his physical control is necessarily limited.

Right here can be seen the fundamental difference between performing and listening—the reason why, although the performer must listen carefully to the music he is making, and the intent listener mentally performs the work he is hearing, the attitudes of the two are dissimilar. The question is one of control. The performer directs, or takes part in the direction of, the course of events in the composition. (Even an orchestral player or a choral singer shares, although to a limited degree, this power of direction. No conductor's power is absolute, and no performer gives up all his individuality.) The listener has no such opportunity; he must submit to the direction of others.

It is important to remember this distinction in considering the interrelationships of performers and auditors. The performer knows, somatically as well as mentally, that he is causing the music; as a result it is easy for him to enjoy a vivid sense of participation. The listener knows equally well that he (the listener) is not producing the music; yet it is not always easy for him to forego that privilege entirely. Hence he may hum, or beat time, or make other physical gestures that simulate actual participation in the performance. Most sophisticated music lovers, however, frankly recognize the limitations of their roles and sublimate their desires for physical activity. At the same time, an imaginary physical involvement underlies the listener's successful identification with the musical persona. For this reason the visual stimulation of watching a performance is important, for observation of the physical gestures of the players can facilitate the empathetic reactions of the auditors to the symbolic gestures of the music. Stravinsky goes so far as to say: "The sight of the gestures and movements of the various parts of the body producing the music is fundamentally necessary if it is to be grasped in all its fullness."[1] Even well-trained musicians may find it hard to concentrate on music in the absence of visual cues, a fact which explains why many of them like, if possible, to follow scores when listening to broadcasts or to recordings.

By deliberately exploiting the dynamic or mechanical as-

[1] *Stravinsky: An Autobiography* (New York: Simon and Schuster, 1936), p. 114.

pects of performance, composers have on occasion emphasized the kinetic-sonic correspondences that underlie instrumental gestures. One who refuses to admit the general truth of Stravinsky's statement would have to grant that it applies to these cases at least. Examples spring to mind: Scarlatti's hand crossings, Bach's open-string pedals for the violin, Ravel's entire Piano Concerto for the Left Hand. In Webern's Piano Variations the play of the two hands against each other—each representing an implied virtual agent—is an essential element of the structure, sometimes clarifying, sometimes counterpointing, the twelve-tone structure and the basic linear directions.

One who knows a piece well can follow a performance in the mind's eye, without actually watching it. But it is precisely the piece that we know well that may elicit our strongest resistance to a new interpretation. We are likely to be especially recalcitrant if we have learned a piece through repeated hearings of a single recording—reiterations that copy one another with an exactitude impossible to any succession of actual performances. (Hence I maintain that one who has learned a piece as a performer or score reader is more receptive to fresh ideas about it than one who has learned it by hearing mechanically literal—and literally mechanical—repetitions.) In order to accept a new reading of a composition we know intimately, we must make an unusually concentrated effort to follow the performance intently, accepting every event just as it comes and resisting the temptation to fight each one by comparing it with a private version. It is certainly easier to do this when we can see as well as hear, when every new detail of interpretation is supported by a visual cue.

In the last analysis what determines acceptance is the quality of the performance itself. The "convincing" interpretation is the one that forces its listener to follow it, no matter whether he knows the piece by heart or has never heard it before. And the convincing performance in this sense is not, I fear, a product of musicianship and musical intelligence alone. Like good acting, it depends on the power of personality; but, as in good acting, the natural personality is converted into a vehicle for the projection of an artistic persona.

The presence of a single commanding figure who sums up and represents the complete musical persona is especially helpful to the average listener in his effort to make contact with that persona. The gestures of such a figure, paralleling those of the music, are easily taken in by the eye; and his position of control enables him to present his conception of the musical gestures forcefully to the ear. These considerations explain at least in part the popularity of virtuoso pianists and conductors on the one hand, and the limited public for chamber music on the other. It is easy to understand, too, why conductors who emphasize their balletic role are so well received. It is not just because of the audience's yearning for sensationalistic titillation; it is at least partly because the balletic conductor, at his best, offers an unusually clear visual analogue of the composite rhythm that controls the music, thus making the complex form more easily comprehensible to the untrained ear.

There is thus nothing reprehensible about taking advantage of the opportunity of reading a performer's gestures as illustrative of the musical design, as long as one does not allow it to take one's attention away from the music itself. I have already discussed one such misdirection of attention: a focus on the person and the personality of the performer himself, rather than on the persona he is projecting. Equally to be avoided is undue concentration on the balletic aspects of the performance to the point where the music becomes a background for the dance. ("I have to sit on the left side where I can watch his fingers.")

Some types of music must be accepted without visual aid

(unless one has recourse to a score). Much electronic music is intrinsically of this variety. At least one branch of instrumental literature, organ music, sometimes belongs to this category for practical reasons: it is often inconvenient if not impossible for many persons to watch an organist as he plays. It is possibly significant that these two kinds of music, although otherwise dissimilar, both tend to emphasize a realistic spatial element in performance. The audience, deprived of visual cues, is encouraged literally to *feel* its identification by an acute sense of its location within an architectural space that is also occupied, traversed, and at times completely filled by the music.

There is one auditor who identifies himself with music in a special way, who responds to it by gesturing not with the hands and feet alone, but with the entire body. I refer, of course, to the dancer, who must be, first if not foremost, a listener. From one point of view, his movements can be seen as a reaction to the music he hears, as an overt version of the imagined or inhibited physical response that music, especially of a "dancelike" nature, often calls forth from its hearers. By one primarily interested in music, then, the dancer's activity can be interpreted as a search for identification with the musical persona through participation in its rhythmic life by means of a dynamic pattern of gestures, a pattern that at the same time may create for an audience a vivid visual analogue to the symbolic gestures of the music.

Serious dancers and balletomanes, however, are primarily interested in dance, not in music. And since their concerns have elicited such a rich musical literature, significant for its contribution not only to the choreographer's art but to the composer's as well, it may be worthwhile to look into the relations between the two arts from their point of view.

The categories of dance in general, as opposed to "the dance" narrowly considered as an art form, show striking correlations to those of song. Thus "natural dance" can be contrasted with "artistic dance." The former includes folk dances, social dances, functional dances of all kinds. Like the natural singer, the natural dancer performs without assuming a dramatic role, frankly hearing the music and frankly dancing. Like natural song, natural dance can be simulated—witness exhibitions of ballroom dancing, for example. In artistic dance, the performer enacts a role, even though it may not be specifically defined in programmatic terms. Thus he does not "hear" the music, nor is he "conscious" of dancing. On the model of singing, his actions are to be interpreted as an intensification of the expressive powers of bodily movement through a subconscious formalization of its rhythmic aspects. (Ritual dance is often a hybrid or borderline case. A participant may assume a role of which he is overtly "conscious." He dances—and perhaps also speaks or sings—simultaneously as a character and in his own person.)

In artistic dance, which is the category that concerns us, what is the relation of the dancer's persona (protagonist, character) to the composer's? Here analogies with song fall down, for, unlike the singer's persona, the dancer's, being visually evoked, cannot be an integral component of the composer's voice. True, the composition of a ballet or other interpretive dance to an already existing piece of music (whether or not the music was written expressly for the purpose) may seem in some ways to resemble the transformation of a purely instrumental composition into a song. Both operations inject a new, personal component—an actual character or set of characters—into a texture that originally comprised only virtual agents. But the protagonist of the song assumes a role in the musical activity by taking over, or at least melodically doubling, the part of one of the agents, which it promotes to the status of a new vocal persona. A superimposed dance, on the other hand, in no way modifies the original musical conception. From the point of view of the music, the role enacted by the dancer is not that of a new persona but of a personification that expresses the rhythmic gestures of the musical persona in visible human form. Yet the dancer as actor or mime does create a persona—a role in the drama, explicit or implicit, of the dance itself. From the point of view of this choreographic character, the music is an accompaniment, an auditory analogue of his bodily movements.

Dance can thus be observed from two opposing directions. The musically oriented members of an audience will tend to see it as a visual enhancement of the music; they will judge it according to the intrinsic interest of the music and the success of the choreography in interpreting its rhythmic structure. For this reason many music lovers are bored or even repelled by ballet, for they often find its accompanying music second-rate, or badly performed, or insufficiently supported by the choreography. Dance lovers of course, will consider the choreographic and histrionic components as primary; they will hear the music as an evocative rhythmic background—but evocative and rhythmic in only the most general sense. Hence they will not worry about its specific musical content or its precise correlation with the choreography.

To be sure, dancers are sometimes accompanied by adequate performances of first-rate music, and some choreography respects the musical rhythm in close detail. One way to achieve such exactitude is by reversing the usual order of composition and devising music to accompany a previously choreographed dance. But if Stravinsky is right, rigid correspondence between musical and choreographic rhythm is undesirable: "Choreography, as I conceive it, must realize its own form, one independent of the musical form, though measured to the musical unit. Its construction will be based on whatever correspondences the choreographer may invent, but it must not seek merely to duplicate the line and beat of the music. I do not see how one can be a choreographer unless, like Balanchine, one is a musician first."[2]

These remarks suggest a third approach to the art of the dance, one that takes seriously both the visual and the auditory components and tries to do justice to the efforts expended by the collaboration of the talents of a Balanchine and a Stravinsky. A ballet such as *Petrouchka* should be viewed neither as a musical composition with personified rhythms, nor as a stage work with musical accompaniment, but as a synthesis of two complementary media. If we think of the dancers as portraying silent characters, who use steps and gestures instead of words, then perhaps we can at last find a fruitful analogy between dance and song. The vocal persona exists on both the conscious verbal and the subconscious musical planes. A character portrayed by a singer is conscious of his words, but he is only subconsciously aware of his melody and its accompaniment. Similarly, the character portrayed by the dancer is conscious of his *actions*, realistically interpreted, but he is only subconsciously aware of his *dancing*, which is both a formalization and an expressive amplification of his natural gestures. In the same way, he is subconsciously aware of his accompaniment, which is at once an audible symbolization of his own gestures and the sonic environment that he shares with the other characters and with the audience. Once we grant this possibility, we can see that dance is open to the same kinds of participation and identification as song, and that ballet, in its own way, can offer the same variety of relationship between character and orchestra as opera. We can identify ourselves with the characters, hearing the music through their (subconscious) ears, or with the rhythmic flow itself, seeing the characters through the eyes of the musical

[2] Igor Stravinsky and Robert Craft, *Memories and Commentaries* (Garden City: Doubleday, 1960), pp. 36–37.

persona. And perhaps it is even possible to discern a complete balletic persona, expressing itself through the synthesis of music and dance—through the constant interplay, no less real for being unconscious, between characters and orchestra. Stravinsky was acutely aware of this interaction, as his account of the genesis of the piece for piano and orchestra that later became *Petrouchka* proves: "In composing the music, I had in my mind a distinct picture of a puppet, suddenly endowed with life, exasperating the patience of the orchestra with diabolical cascades of arpeggios. The orchestra in turn retaliates with menacing trumpet blasts. The outcome is a terrific noise which reaches its climax and ends in the sorrowful and querulous collapse of the poor puppet."[3]

Background music for cinema, when composed with serious attention to the drama it supports, has some points in common with ballet, although it can be argued that if such music is really successful it will be only, or almost, subliminally apprehended by the audience. I doubt whether this is ever actually the case; in point of fact, the music often becomes so obtrusive that the motion picture suffers from a divided attention similar to that afflicting melodrama. When it is adequately individualized yet at the same time sufficiently subordinated to the action, however, background music can induce us, as members of the audience, to participate more thoroughly in the life of the cinema than we otherwise might. As in opera, the music can create an environment that we share with the characters portrayed. We often feel the need of this illusion, even in talking pictures, for the screen produces the effect of a separate world that we know we can never enter. By binding us together with the inhabitants of that world, the music convinces us of its reality. Sometimes we can interpret it as referring to the subconscious

[3] *Autobiography*, p. 48.

life of the characters; often, however, it seems to have a more general function, attaching itself as it were to the psyche of the camera-eye itself. Skillfully handled, it can encourage us to identify ourselves with that camera-eye, which represents the point of view of the film maker—or better, of his persona. It is obvious why conscientious directors are careful, even chary of its use: no musical aid to identification would be better than a misleading one. Advanced film makers no longer regard music as an embellishment added to an otherwise complete film. They conceive of the total sound track, which may be partly— or even entirely—musical, as a structural component of a cinematic work that addresses itself simultaneously to eye and ear.

The foregoing discussion suggests that music, even when it is specifically designed to be narrowly functional, still exerts its influence in the direction of participation and identification. Indeed, one might claim that this is precisely what the function of functional music usually is; whenever music is used as background or accompaniment, as part of a service or celebration, as encouragement of patriotism or religiosity or pure conviviality —in all these cases it works through its power to unite those who hear it as joint participants in a common enterprise. Through the music they more easily identify themselves as members of a group adopting the attitude, or engaged in the activity, symbolized by the music.

To be sure, one can resist this power. One can listen to music objectively; one can even perform it objectively. But should one? Obviously one may have strong reasons for resisting the identification suggested by functional music—at gatherings designed to whip up fanatic emotionalism, for example. The question I am raising here, however, concerns our response to music as an art. And I realize that many composers, performers, and music lovers would insist that an attitude of impersonal observation leads more surely to musical understanding than the active participation I have been describing and, at least by implication, recommending.

Objective or impersonal performance is not to be confused with mechanical playing. Mechanical playing is unconscious playing: it occurs during the trancelike state familiar to all musicians who have learned their parts so well that their fingers will play without the intervention of their minds. No; by impersonal performance I mean not unconscious but hyperconscious playing (or singing): performance that the musician has achieved, not through a search for personal identification, but by structural analysis directed toward projecting the composition in question as an objectively perceptible shape, or by research aimed at the reconstruction of the work as a historical document. Similarly, the impersonal listener resists the temptation of identification at any level; he tries to perceive the work as a structural pattern or as the exemplification of a historical style rather than to participate in it as an experience. (If he is really thorough-going, he probably prefers what he hears when he reads the score to himself, for few performances are likely to be rigorously objective enough to satisfy him.) One who employs the impersonal approach need not deny that a composition is a dramatic construct, but his interest in its components depends on their structural interrelationships or their historical connotations and not on his personal involvement.

One objective approach is thus the analytical approach. It characterizes an important stage in the comprehension of any work, whether on the part of a performer or of a listener, but it is ideally neither the first nor the last stage. Some kind of personal contact with a piece must precede analysis; how else is one to know what, if anything, it contains that is of interest? Ideally, personal contact should follow analysis, for the aim of music is to provide intense experiences, not structures for contemplation.

Analysis, then, should follow and grow out of one's intuitive grasp of a composition. It is often useful when one has achieved an identification that is successful and complete to the point of boredom, when one knows a piece so well that it is impossible to pretend that it contains any surprises or affords any suspense. At this point, only the objective perspective of an analysis can inform one whether the piece conceals possibilities of its own renewal, or whether it must remain, for the time being at least, played out. Even in the latter case, analysis often enables a composition otherwise dead to continue to afford pleasure as a beautifully constructed design, or as the solution of an interesting compositional problem.

Analysis is perhaps still more fruitful when one's identification is tantalizingly imperfect: when one feels that a composition works but cannot figure out how or why it works; or when an otherwise enjoyable piece is marred by one or two details that prevent one's complete immersion in its flow. Now one engages in analysis, not because one knows the piece too well, but because one does not know it well enough. One is sure that the desired identification is possible and hopes that analysis will show how it is to be achieved. If one fails, one can still enjoy the composition, although incompletely—hoping, perhaps, to hear one day an extraordinary performance that will uncover the missing connections.

Most satisfying of all is the interpenetration of analysis and identification that characterizes one's response to music of the highest quality. At every stage of one's acquaintance with such music, new questions arise to be submitted to analysis; and every exercise of analysis reveals new opportunities for enriched participation.

An illustrative example will show this process at work. Since it is based on well-known facts about a familiar composition, it will reveal no startlingly original insights; but it has the merit of autobiographical accuracy. When I first learned to play Beethoven's Sonata in E Op. 109 I found myself easily caught up in the exciting sweep of the last variation of the finale, which rises to an obvious climax of intensity, speed, and register, be fore sinking into the benedictory recapitulation of the theme. It was not until much later that I began to wonder about the diminished seventh (on E-sharp) that ushers in the climactic plateau of thirty-second-note figuration over the extended dominant trill (mm. 168–169): why was this chord, an interloper in the key of E, so right? At that point analysis came to my aid, pointing out that the chord culminates a series of events set in motion by a detail in the second variation: the D-naturals that mysteriously replace the dominant in the first measure of the second half of the theme (m. 57). This new note is explained in its immediate context by the resolution that follows, and together with that resolution it forms a recurring motif in the subsequent variations. It returns harmonically amplified in Variation IV (mm. 104–105 bis) and contrapuntally developed in Variation V (mm. 129 and 137). Realizing this, I could hear the climactic diminished seventh as introducing the last episode in the fortunes of the D-natural, just as I could also hear, in the final section of the variation, its echo beneath the original motif it had tried to displace (m. 177). Armed with this new knowledge, I could recognize in the variations a more organic unity than before, and I derived increased satisfaction from the diminished seventh chord that had set me off on my investigation (Ex. 8).

Now, however, it suddenly struck me that this sonority was not unique to the climactic point, or to the finale. Almost precisely the same sound had been used to introduce the recapitu-

8. Beethoven, Sonata Op. 109, last movement. The beginning of the second half of the theme is shown, and the corresponding measures in several of the variations.

lation of the second subject of the first movement. Analysis intervened again, this time revealing that the section of the finale introduced by the diminished seventh presented a transfigured return of that subject (Ex. 9). This was the event that all those

D-naturals had been promising! But there was more to come. Taking the hint offered by the relationship between the second half of the final variation and the second subject of the first movement, I now looked for a corresponding connection between the first half of the variation and the first subject. It was not hard to find, for it was suggested by the chordal layout of the variation (Ex. 10). In sum, the last variation exposed beneath the division of the sonata into movements a hidden unity of structure based on the reflection of the two subjects of the

opening movement in the two halves of the theme of the finale.
Here indeed was a pattern that I could contemplate with delight; more important—and more profoundly enjoyable—was
my new feeling, while playing the sonata, that I could experi-

9. Beethoven, Sonata Op. 109, last and first movements. The climax
of the last variation is to be compared with the second subject of the
opening movement, here shown as it appears in the recapitulation.

ence it and project it as a single broad gesture.[4] I realized that
my previous attempts at participation had been inadequate,
owing to my incomplete comprehension of the motivations of
the sonata's musical energy. The identifications hitherto avail-

---

[4] For further discussion, from somewhat different points of view, of the
connections among the movements of this sonata, see Allen Forte, *The Compositional Matrix* (Baldwin, N. Y.: Music Teachers' National Association,
1961); also Philip Barford, "The Piano Music—II," in Denis Arnold and Nigel
Fortune, eds., *The Beethoven Reader* (New York: Norton, 1971), pp. 171–174.

able to me, based on a sectional, movement-by-movement view of the form, had been partial and even fragmentary compared with the all-embracing one now possible.

A parallel argument could be developed about the values and limitations of an objective historical approach to music. Some historians have a tendency to consider compositions more as documents of the past than as works of art. The best scholars, however, recognize that only as a composition speaks to us as a work of art can we comprehend its full value as a historical document. At the same time, only as the result of extensive and thorough historical investigations has much of the music of the past become available to our experience. Only in this way have we been able to arrive at an adequate conception of its sound

10. Beethoven, Sonata Op. 109, last and first movements. Here the opening of the last variation is to be compared with the first measures of the sonata.

and sense, of how it should be played and how it should be heard. So here, as in analysis, the objective and personal responses must interpenetrate each other, and this is equally true whether one wishes ultimately to use the music to illuminate the past or the past to illuminate the music.

The same interpenetration is essential to the activity of music criticism, whether of composition or of performance. The critic of any work of art should aim toward helping his readers to make personal contact with that work and to experience it in the ways that the critic considers relevant to its comprehension. It follows that he cannot criticize a work that he has not vividly experienced himself. A critic of a musical composition, then, must begin with his own sense of participation and identification. His criticism can then try to gain a wider perspective, based on an analytical and perhaps historical view of the composition.

Valid criticism of performance likewise depends on the critic's objective knowledge and personal experience of the work in question. A complete criticism must try to do justice to a performance from the points of view of its structural clarity (as determined by analysis), its stylistic propriety (as determined by historical provenance), and its cogency (as determined by the critic's own experience of identification). The only occasion on which a critic might legitimately discuss the playing of an unfamiliar composition would be the performance of a work whose style and form are second nature to him; in that case his experience of the work might be almost automatic, and he could concentrate his attention on the interpretation. Yet how many times do we read, in essence, "The composition was completely incomprehensible, but it was beautifully played"!

Criticism, then, like analysis and historical scholarship, must be based on an intuitive personal response, which in turn may be deepened in perception and heightened in intensity by study. It might still be argued, however, that this response does not require the sense of identification that I have been expounding. Perhaps there are other ways of participating in the life of a composition. One does not, for example, have to walk around in a depicted scene in order to appreciate it—although such an imaginary activity often seems the most appropriate response to Chinese landscapes. Or one can read a novel without identifying oneself with one of the characters. If I am repelled by the narrator of *A Clockwork Orange*, I need not place myself inside his skin, or even within his world; I can simply listen to him talk. Perhaps that is what we usually do when we read novels or go to plays: listen to others talk. True, by becoming actors, openly or at heart, we can let literature speak *through* us. More often, however, it speaks *to* us, and frequently we are only eavesdropping.

All this may be granted; yet it does not affect the argument with regard to music. For the response demanded by music is different from that demanded by the other arts, and the nature of that difference goes far toward explaining the extraordinary power that music seems to exert over our inner life. We do not, after all, inhabit the depicted space of a painting; even our walk in the Chinese landscape is imaginary, not real. We do not occupy the actual space of a statue. We do not live inside the minds of characters. But music creates an environment that all share, for it surrounds and permeates all equally; it unifies characters, agents, and auditors in a single world of sound. That is why music, unlike poetry, can speak *to* us only as it speaks *through* us. (Architecture similarly creates an all-embracing environment, a space common to buildings and those who use them. It is for this reason, rather than for fancied similarities between architectural and musical form, that the art deserves its hackneyed sobriquet.)

Zerlina admirably symbolizes the situation. When she responds to Don Giovanni's initial advances in "Là ci darem," her words reply, consciously and reasonably, to his suggestion. But her melody, her subconscious reaction, reflects his. Already, long before she gives in verbally, she has identified herself with his point of view; thus she appropriates his music, remaking it in accordance with her own style. Later, when the flute doubles Don Giovanni's voice in the recapitulation, can we not take it as an audible representation of her whole-hearted participation in his melodic line, just as the bassoon that doubles her answer can be assumed to reveal the extent of his identification with hers (Ex. 5 and 11)?

11. Mozart, *Don Giovanni,* "Là ci darem la mano." This is the reprise of the theme reproduced in Ex. 5. In the exposition, Zerlina's statement is a slightly extended variation of Don Giovanni's. Now, in the reprise, the two are brought even closer together. Zerlina follows Don Giovanni after only two measures, completing his phrase. Moreover, the flute now doubling his statement in a higher register prepares for her entry, just as the bassoon doubling her own part continues his line below.

Don Giovanni's words thus speak *to* Zerlina—to her conscious faculties; his music speaks *through* her—through her subconscious sense of personal participation. Zerlina's subconscious reaction to the music as portrayed in the drama reflects our conscious experience of the art in actual life. When we listen to words we can think about them, around them, forward and back, even while we follow them. When we listen to music, whether with words or not, we must follow it as if it were our own thought. We are bound to it—to its tempo, to its progression, to its dynamics. We can recall the past or foresee the future only as they are reflected in our awareness of each moment of the perpetually flowing present. And if that awareness is sufficiently acute, and our attention sufficiently constant, we can succeed in feeling that we have *become* the music, or that the music has become ourselves. Perhaps, then, my original disclaimer of any mystical content in the concept of identification was too sweeping. The apprehension of the unity of the musical work, and of the union of work with self, is clearly analogous to the experience reported by the mystic of his relations with the One.

Edmund Gurney finds this sense of identity peculiarly applicable to our reactions to melody:

> There is one characteristic of melody which attention to its aspect as motion brings out with special clearness; and that is our sense of entire oneness with it, of its being as it were a mode of our own life. We feel in it, indeed, an objective character, inasmuch as we instinctively recognise that it has for others the same permanent possibilities of impression as for ourselves; but our sense of it nevertheless is not as of an external presentation, but of something evolved within ourselves by a special activity of our own.[5]

But what Gurney says here of melody can be applied to musical progression as a whole; he himself implicitly makes this generalization when he suggests that "we may feel, at the end of a musical movement, that we have been living an engrossing piece of life."[6]

One bit of evidence for this view is the music that many of us—including, I should think, all musicians—constantly carry around inside our heads. It comes to us, unbidden, when we wake up in the morning and remains with us all day during our conscious moments, except when masked by louder sounds. We can let it have its way, or we can direct it to our will; we can force it into new paths, or we can rehearse familiar works; we can listen to it, or we can relegate it to our subconscious; but we can never get rid of it. For one so endowed—or so burdened— to live is to live music. To compose is to control this inner voice, to shape it into new forms, to make it speak for us. To listen to music is to yield our inner voice to the composer's domination. Or better: it is to make the composer's voice our own.

[5] Edmund Gurney, *The Power of Sound* (New York: Basic Books, 1966), p. 166.
[6] Ibid., p. 347.

8

Epilogue: Utterance and Gesture

Even the most sympathetic reader of the foregoing pages will no doubt be dissatisfied, and on two counts. In the first place, he may contend that the discussion primarily develops an elaborate figure of speech, and that conclusions based on analogies cannot be trusted.

He would be right. Yet I do not see how an attempt to interpret nonverbal and unverbalizable phenomena can proceed otherwise than by metaphor and analogy. No doubt, at every point along the way I should have posted a little sign reading So To Speak, or As It Were, but this would soon have proved tiresome to the reader. So I depend on his indulgence, hoping that I have not used my metaphors illegitimately. It is true that argument of this kind cannot lead to conclusions as firm as those of deductive logic, but it is not true that it cannot lead to reasonable and even convincing conclusions. Its method is not proof but persuasion. So, although I freely grant that I have proved nothing, I hope that I have persuaded some readers of the reasonableness of some of the results of my investigations.

The second hypothetical complaint refers to subject matter, not method. Here is a book, one may say, that apparently promises to deal with music as a medium of communication. Yet it never comes to grips, except briefly and almost peripherally, with the basic question of what music means or expresses.

To this charge, too, I plead guilty; and again the guilt is deliberately incurred. The subject of my study is not what music is about but rather how one might profitably think about music. More specifically, my task has been to consider what it means to say that music is a form of utterance, and not to determine what such utterance might be trying to say. A number of interesting essays on the latter subject—sometimes called musical semantics—have appeared over the past few years.[1] These differ widely from one another in their methods and in their conclusions, but all of them seem either to ignore problems that I deem basic to all such investigations, or to take their solutions for granted.

My study, then, is meant to be prefatory to any theory of musical meaning or musical expression, and I have tried to keep it broad enough to serve as a framework for almost any such theory—even that of the pure formalist. For most of the categories of my dramatistic analysis, as I have pointed out, become formal categories when observed from another point of view. The formalist need only reinterpret them thus in the case of absolute music. The extramusical implications of program music he can dismiss as illusory, and he can insist that the verbal expression of song is only conventionally associated with the music. Or, applying a more sophisticated technique, he can look in both program and text for patterns that, by their relations to the purely musical design, can add a new dimension of structural complexity.

It should be clear, though, that I do not accept the formalist's premises; and at this point it is perhaps only fair to state what my own are. I do so tentatively, for these matters are highly speculative. I put forward the following, then, as the view that seems to me the most reasonable at the moment.

My investigation has developed the picture of music as a

---

[1] E.g.: Wilson Coker, *Music and Meaning* (New York: The Free Press, 1972); Donald N. Ferguson, *Music and Metaphor* (Minneapolis: University of Minnesota Press, 1960); Terence McLaughlin, *Music and Communication* (London: Faber and Faber, 1970); Leonard B. Meyer, *Emotion and Meaning in Music* (Chicago: University of Chicago Press, 1956).

form of utterance, to be compared and contrasted with the verbal utterances of ordinary speech and of imaginative literature. If a sample of ordinary speech is an actual utterance, then a literary production is a simulated utterance: it is not to be construed as the utterance of a real person, living or dead, but as that of a persona or character who is an imaginary creation of the literary work itself—indeed, who subsists only by virtue of the literary utterance. (One could make a further distinction between simulated utterances on the page and in performance —as read and as heard. But, as in music, reading is a kind of performance, albeit a silent one. Hence I find the distinction unnecessary. In this connection one must remember that the performed utterance is not the utterance of the performer, but of the character he portrays.)

The medium of musical utterance, like that of speech, consists of purposefully organized sounds, produced or producible by actual performers. But except in the special case of natural song, the utterances themselves, like those of literature, are artistic creations to be construed as simulated—as emanating from personas or characters who subsist only by virtue of the musical composition. But musical sounds, unlike those of speech, are basically nonverbal. Song, of course, makes use of verbal utterance; but even in unaccompanied song one can distinguish between the verbal and vocal levels of expression. Qua poetry, a song is a kind of verbal utterance; qua music, its medium is the human voice, independent of verbal meaning— a vocal, symbolic, nonverbal utterance. Instrumental music, whether alone or accompanying the voice, goes one step further in the direction of abstraction from the word and constitutes a form of purely symbolic utterance, an utterance by analogy with song.

Has musical utterance any meaning? The answer naturally depends on what one means by "meaning," and what one means by the question. For example, it can be contended that no piece of music has a meaning because no work of art has a meaning—*a* meaning, of which one can say, "This is the meaning of the work of art." For, although a work of art may have meaning, or meanings, it is never its function—as it is the function of a piece of expository prose—merely to convey information that can be identified as its meaning.

The question whether music has meaning is usually intended, however, to compare or to contrast music with poetry, not with expository prose. A poem, whether or not it has *a* meaning, normally has both meaning—that is, paraphrasable content—and meanings—that is, the connotations and denotations of its words and phrases. On both counts music fails. True, music has its own syntax. But it has no content that can be paraphrased in other music, or in words, or in any other medium; and its elements—notes, chords, motifs—normally have no referents. (Here, of course, is where the metaphor of music as a language completely fails.)

One might offer Wagner's leitmotifs as counterexamples; but the objects, characters, etc., with which the motifs are associated hardly ever function analogously to semantic referents. In some cases, the musical idea has merely been *named* in accordance with a presumable dramatic counterpart. That is, if a motif is frequently associated with dramatic situations involving X, and if the motif sounds expressively appropriate to X, then it is convenient to give it the same name as X. This is the case with many of Wagner's motifs, the names of which vary from commentator to commentator according to their interpretations of the situations in question. In other examples, the musical idea seems to have been designed as a suggestive *representation* of X. But such a representation no more *means* X than a portrait *means* its sitter. As usual, Berlioz is on the right track. The musical *idée fixe* of the *Fantastic Symphony* is a melody that is always associated in the mind of the hero with the image of his beloved. Whenever he thinks of her, the melody appears. But the melodic image in his mind's ear does not *mean* "the Beloved" any more than the visual image in his mind's eye does.

To be sure, once one has accepted a definite name for a motif, it is hard to keep from thinking of that name whenever the motif is sounded. The referent of the name does then become an artificial referent of the motif. Exploitation of this reaction can lead to a kind of arbitrary symbolism that some composers have deliberately employed—usually at the expense of more typically musical values. Even Berlioz may have gone too far in this direction when he inserted the *idée fixe* at the end of the "March to the Scaffold." Certainly Strauss relied on the method in the mechanical exposition of leitmotifs in his melodrama "Enoch Arden." So did Puccini when he allowed the conventional associations of a familiar theme to inform his audience of the nationality of *Madama Butterfly*'s hero-villain. To most listeners today, "Enoch Arden" seems overly contrived, and Puccini's use of "The Star-Spangled Banner" downright ludicrous. Referents may thus be attached to musical ideas, but always at the risk of doing violence to the medium.

Words do not always have referents. "Hey-diddle-diddle" is a word, or phrase, used in a well-known poem, but it is entirely meaningless. We need not restrict ourselves to nonsense syllables. Words like "oh" and "ah," while perfectly intelligible in context, have no core of meaning that can be independently conveyed. "Oh" can express astonishment, delight, regret, fear, and so on. That is, in context the single word can mean "I am astonished," "I am delighted," "I am sorry," or "I am afraid." Although these shades of meaning can be indicated to some extent by a speaker's tone of voice, they can be interpreted with certainty only by one who is familiar with the context. In this sense, then, words like "oh" and "ah" are meaningless—but meaningful! They function as pure gesture—to borrow a term used by R. P. Blackmur.[2] For language has a gestural as well as a strictly semantic aspect. Semantically a verbal utterance conveys a conceptual content; gesturally, it functions as an expressive action. Like physical gesture, verbal gesture communicates the speaker's (or the writer's) attitude toward what he is saying; or it tries to influence his hearers (or readers), not by the sense of the discourse, but by its intensity.

Especially in dramatic poetry, even words of normal signification can be used to produce almost pure gestural effects that depend less on the specific meanings of the words than on the modes of performance—the kinds of expression—they imply. This is true, for example, in those reiterative passages so characteristic of Shakespeare, in which a word or phrase will be repeated long after it has done its semantic work, or even without regard for that work. The context determines the tempo, the tone of voice, and the inflections, that must be used in order to convey the appropriate intensity, for the words in themselves reveal little. Such passages as the following are merely silly when presented in isolation:

"Tomorrow, and tomorrow, and tomorrow . . ."

"Howl, howl, howl, howl!"

"Never, never, never, never, never!"

Yet in context they are extremely powerful, for they articulate attitudes that are usually only suggested by half-articulate interjections, or else relegated to the realm of the completely inarticulate—sighs, groans, cries of pain, snarls of rage. A level of half-conscious, almost involuntary utterance is raised to the level of fully realized poetic expression.

2 See the title essay in R. P. Blackmur, *Language as Gesture* (New York: Harcourt Brace, 1952), pp. 3–24. My discussion is greatly indebted to Blackmur's.

Not all poetry, and very little prose, can exploit the potentialities of language as gesture to the extent of the quoted passages. But the gestural aspect is often present when unsuspected —concealed, perhaps, in the syntax or the word order. In the best poetry—in the best prose, for that matter—gesture and meaning complement and reinforce each other.

It is the gestural aspect of utterance that is simulated, and symbolized, by music. If music is a language at all, it is a language of gesture: of direct actions, of pauses, of startings and stoppings, of rises and falls, of tenseness and slackness, of accentuations. These gestures are symbolized by musical motifs and progressions, and they are given structure by musical rhythm and meter, under the control of musical tempo. The vocal utterance of song emphasizes, even exaggerates, the gestural potentialities of its words. Instrumental utterance, lacking intrinsic verbal content, goes so far as to constitute what might be called a medium of pure symbolic gesture.

The gestures of music can be interpreted as symbolic of physical as well as verbal gestures. For a physical gesture is an action that emulates an utterance— an action that tries to speak (hence our admiration of the "eloquent gesture"). If music resembles utterance in being sound, it resembles physical gesture in being speechless. Once more, in music symbolic utterance and symbolic gesture come together. Indeed, in music symbolic utterance *is* symbolic gesture.

Another way of putting the same point is to say that music is both poetry and dance. This is not meant to imply a theory of the origin of music, but to suggest that in music both the verbal gestures of poetry and the bodily gestures of the dance are symbolized in the medium of pure sound. The present study has approached its subject mainly from the direction of poetry. No doubt a similar investigation could start with the dance. I should expect it to come to similar conclusions.

The symbolic gestures of music, like the verbal gestures cited above, are both meaningless and meaningful. This apparent contradiction arises, of course, from a play on words. In the same spirit we might also say: musical gestures lack signification, but they can be significant. Like a sigh, a musical gesture has no specific referent, it conveys no specific message. But like a sigh, it can prove appropriate to many occasions; it can fit into many contexts, which in return can explain its significance. The expressive content of the musical gesture, then, depends on its context. Deprived of context, the gesture expresses nothing; it is only potentially expressive.

No context, no content. Almost all musicians would agree with this dictum when interpreted in a strictly formal way to mean that only the syntactical and formal context supplied by a specific compositional situation can reveal the significance of a musical idea. Only the die-hard Wagnerian would maintain the contrary. But I mean something stronger. Significance must include the significance of the entire composition as well as of each motif. And content refers to humanly expressive content. I use that somewhat pretentious term for want of a better. "Emotional content" is too restrictive, and it begs the question of what music expresses. "Extramusical content" implies something adventitious, not really connected with the music. So I come back to "humanly expressive content": whatever of human importance a musical composition may express, not only through each individual gesture, but also through the totality of gestures that constitutes its form. "No context, no content," then, means: a composition represents a human action, and only in a context of wider human activity is its content revealed.

Context in this sense is most obviously provided by words that are actually sung. These can, for example, tell us whether a musical sigh—perhaps a downward slur—is one of relief or of despondency. They can define the change of mood implied by a modulation. They can explain a rapid movement as the result of impetuosity, or fear, or sheer good spirits. They can, in short, associate each musical motion with a human emotion—or mood, or activity, or attitude. When the gestures of the music are closely analogous to those implied by the words, we are tempted to say that the music expresses the emotion, mood, activity, or attitude revealed by the text. Perhaps it does, but if so only contingently, not necessarily. It would therefore be more accurate to say that the music appropriates the emotion, etc., of the text, and through this borrowed meaning it realizes some part of its expressive potential. (Yet the music pays well for the privilege, as I point out in chapter 2.) It is thus wrong to conclude that the emotion—or any other state of mind, idea, or image, derived from the poetry—constitutes the content of the song. The content emerges from the mutual relations of words and musical gestures, and from the light they throw on each other. A song is thus a kind of metaphor, an equation whose significance consists, not in what it states about either of the two members, but in the coupling itself—in the fact that the equality is asserted.

The suggestion that music does not express emotions but appropriates them gains some plausibility from the existence of strophic song—one might say, with reference to examples from *Die schöne Müllerin,* the triumphant existence. The fact that a given musical setting can be applied to a number of different stanzas need not mean that the music is expressively neutral, since for any of the Schubert examples it would be easy to find stanzas that would fit metrically but would not work because of expressive disparity. What strophic song suggests is that a piece of music allows a wide but not unrestricted range of possible expression: this is what I call its expressive potential. A given text specifies one possibility, or at most a relatively narrow range of possibility, its verbal formulation providing the immediate context that renders the musical gestures emotionally, etc., expressive.

At the same time, a text can do something more. Its content—the states of mind, ideas, and images it communicates—can be taken as an example of the kind of human content that can properly be associated with the music; and by this exemplification it can suggest a broad span of the entire range of expression available to that music. In a successful strophic song, every stanza offers such an example, each throwing its own light on the whole field of the expressive potential.

Words, then, do not limit the potential of music; rather, by specification and exemplification, they may render it more easily comprehensible. The situation is not very different when the words are only implied, as in chorale-preludes or transcriptions. The connotations of a known text and of its associated melody can be just as vivid to the informed listener as if they were actually being sung.

Another way in which music can be supplied with a human context is by a program, and the most convincing justification of program music rests on an argument similar to the preceding. A program can specify a general mood to be associated with the movement of the music, or it can follow—or direct—the course of the music more closely through the succession of sounds, actions, tensions, and relaxations that its narrative suggests. The effectiveness of a program depends on the degree to which it is felt to be figuratively isomorphic with the form of the composition—the extent to which the pattern of activity suggested by the program corresponds to the pattern of symbolic gestures created by the music. Naturally, the less detailed the program is, the easier it is for the listener to imagine such correspondence. This is probably the reason why composers who do not normally utilize explicit programs are willing to imply vague ones by suggestive titles: Funeral March, Ballade, Nocturne, and the like.

To what extent does the program influence the content of the composition? The content of song is to be found in the mutual illumination of text and music; but there the words are an integral part of the complete composition. The music, that is to say, is heard in a specific verbal context. A program, however, is merely an adjunct to the music with which it is associated. Words and music are not sounded together; and since they are not synchronized, it is fruitless even to try to imagine them as sounding together. In fact, the exact words are of little importance; the program consists of the ideas the words convey. A program, then, gives a composition a conceptual, not a verbal, context. Its content, like that of a song text, can serve as an example of the expressive possibilities of the music. But whereas the words of the song provide a context that is both specifically relevant to the music and exemplary, the context provided by the program is only exemplary. That is why it is usually considered a fault to include in a composition details that are related only programmatically to the structure as a whole. These fasten on the composition an interpretation that should be at most suggestive of the total expressive potential.

An example or two may clarify this point. Debussy has given us every encouragement, by his title and by his directions to the pianist, to hear "Des pas sur la neige" as depicting a wintry landscape. But one can imagine a number of other desolate scenes to which the music would be equally appropriate. Or one can think in more abstract terms of loneliness and regret. Finally, one can simply try to let the music communicate its expressive message through one's subconscious associations with its symbolic gestures. If one applies these levels of abstraction to "Feux d'artifice," however, one is always brought up short by the quotation from "La Marseillaise" at the end. Here is a formally gratuitous detail that gains significance most readily from the assumption that the piece really depicts the fireworks at a public celebration, and that we hear the music of a band dying away in the distance. On this literal level the passage is effective and amusing, but it limits the possible significance of the music and discourages one from taking it very seriously.

The best program music, in other words, can be heard as absolute music. Absolute music is music with no specific verbal context, but this does not mean that it lacks context. As in the more abstract approaches to program music, so here each listener supplies his own context, out of the store of his own experience. He may do this consciously and verbally, finding in the first movement of Beethoven's Fifth Symphony a struggle against Fate, and in the finale a triumphant victory. Such interpretations, however, often divert one's attention from the course of the music. Moreover, one tends to take one's own interpretation as more than merely exemplary, and to consider it as the true context—even the true content—of the music. More sophisticated listeners therefore eschew such verbalization. Many of them claim to enjoy music as pure structure alone. I doubt whether this is ever possible, for even when our conscious attention is entirely occupied with following the formal design, our subconscious, in Proustian fashion, is still creating a context—nonverbal but highly personal. We subconsciously ascribe to the music a content based on the correspondence between musical gestures and their patterns on the one hand, and isomorphically analogous experiences, inner or outer, on the other. So long as we do not—or cannot—express these experiences or explain their correspondence with the music in words, we cannot be tempted to maintain that they restrictively define the context of the composition. The danger is rather that, unaware of the power of this level of musical comprehension, we adopt the formalist position. But is this so dangerous after all? The claim of the strict formalist is but the extreme version of an important truth: that only by concentrating on the structure of a composition can we allow our subconscious complete freedom to adduce, from its fund of knowledge and experience, the appropriate associations that will suggest, by exemplification, the full range of the composition's expressive potential.

This view seems reasonable in the light of a situation familiar to many music lovers. Few of us try to define our reactions to a given composition in terms of mood or emotion, but whenever we are asked point-blank to do so, we discover that our subconscious has already done the job. We know what the piece is "about," and we know that we know, but we usually have to grope for a way to express it. Often the verbalization we come up with will not be abstract but related to specific kinds of personal experience.

Sometimes the principle works in the opposite direction. Young pianists often fail to give convincing accounts of the last Beethoven sonatas not because of technical deficiency or lack of intellectual understanding but because of insufficient emotional maturity. Their personal histories offer them no parallel to help them gauge the expressive potential of the music. And it not infrequently happens—as attested by more than one eminent musician—that in the course of events one encounters situations that startlingly illuminate, and are illuminated by, such a composition hitherto imperfectly grasped. For our musical sensibility is affected by our experience—and not just our musical experience. The capacity for seemingly perpetual self-renewal that characterizes the greatest music is only partially due to the fact that we keep finding in it new patterns of structural relationships; in fact, this is not always the case. But we do, continually though subconsciously, bring new personal experiences to bear on it, finding in them new exemplifications of an ever-widening range of expressive possibilities.

Because each listener's reconstruction of the human context must be in terms of his own experience, attempts at verbal formulation of that context vary—sometimes widely. Nor, if we could read the subconscious reactions of which the words are only imperfect and incomplete reports, would we find any more unanimity. This does not condemn us to complete relativism, however. For the context is not the content, it is only the necessary vehicle of the content. The content of a song is not revealed by the words alone but by the quasi-metaphorical relation between words and music. In the same way, the content of instrumental music is revealed to each listener by the relation between the music and the personal context he brings to it. Since each such context can be only exemplary, the resulting content can be only partial. The total content of a complex and profound composition is thus probably beyond the comprehension of any individual listener; it is a potential content matching the entire expressive potential. If the context a hearer adduces is related to the composition analogically, through isomorphic resemblance to its gestures and their structural pattern, and not adventitiously, through arbitrary choice or chance connection, then that context will contribute legitimately and appropriately to the total potential. Superficially divergent as one listener's context may seem from another's, they will be linked by their common isomorphism with the musical structure, and hence with each other. And deeper analysis should reveal, beneath the surface differences, some common ground of expression that in turn suggests the nature of the complete potential. Here, finally, is where the total potential content of any musical work is located: in the relationship among all its contexts and in the illumination thrown on that relationship by the musical structure that unites them.

It is therefore possible for a complex work like Mozart's Symphony No. 40 to receive such diverse, even contradictory characterizations as "heroically tragic"[3] and "[exhibiting] the poised gracefulness of Greece."[4] We must assume that any serious listener who reports a reaction of this kind has brought to bear on his interpretation those of his own experiences that seem to fit the patterns of the music. Owing to a combination of temperament and personal history, one such listener may find that the sum of the adduced associations suggests heroism in defeat; for the same reasons, another invokes an image of contentment in a classical setting. If we could examine and analyze the relevant experiences of both, we should no doubt come to the conclusion that the common ground of context uniting them and relating them to the music is not necessarily attached to any mood. It might, for example, be a pattern of restrained impulses and controlled energies, which some may associate with tragic resignation and others with temperate joy. A more philosophically disposed listener might recognize both possibilities. For him the content of the movement would derive from the discovery of the basic likenesses revealed by the music as underlying two apparently opposed states of mind. Even this would be a partial content, however. A still more profound view of the movement might find its expressive potential in a general attitude applicable to a broad spectrum of moods and emotional reactions—for example, an essential serenity despite superficial agitation, based on a realistic acceptance of whatever comes. Yet even this might not yield the total content. The expressive potential of Mozart's music is so broad that

[3] Albert Einstein, *Mozart, His Character, His Work,* trans. Arthur Mendel and Nathan Broder (New York: Oxford University Press, 1945), p. 235.

[4] "Nun vergleiche man die Mozartsche G-moll-Symphonie, diese griechisch-schwebende Grazie," Robert Schumann, "Characteristik der Tonarten," in *Gesammelte Schriften über Musik und Musiker,* 5th edition, Martin Kreisig, ed. (Leipzig: Breitkopf und Härtel, 1914), Vol. I, p. 105.

one understands immediately what W. J. Turner has in mind when he compares it to "a still, bright, perfect, cloudless day. . . . Such a day does not provoke or in the faintest degree suggest one mood rather than another. It is infinitely protean. It means just what you mean. It is intangible, immaterial—fitting your spirit like a glove."[5]

For the musician, the fact that he can never satisfactorily formulate the content of a composition in words is no disadvantage. Why should he try? For him the gestures of music are second nature. They are a part of his subconscious as well as his conscious mind. They are, in fact, an important segment of that store of experience that subconsciously creates a context for music. For the musician, that is, the context created by his memory is largely, although never entirely, a musical context. When he tries to verbalize the significance of a certain composition, he often does so by relating it to other musical works.

In a more general sense, the same is true of every informed listener. In order to understand any piece of music, he must place it in the context of a musical style and its conventions— again, by relating it to other works. When he cannot make such connections, as when an untrained Westerner hears music of the Orient, he fails to recognize the content, or else he grossly misinterprets it.

The formalist goes one step further and insists that the only context, or the only legitimate context, of music is other music. For him its apparent human content is factitious, arising solely from the traditional and arbitrary associations of stylistic convention. But such generalization is unwarranted. True, musical expression does rely heavily on convention, but music is not alone among the arts in this respect. An appreciation of their conventional aspects is essential to an understanding of

[5] W. J. Turner, *Mozart: The Man and His Works* (New York: Knopf, 1938), pp. 380–381.

all of them—even of the verbal and representational arts, to which the power of expressing human content is usually conceded. For stylistic conventions are not necessarily arbitrary. They arise for both expressive and formal reasons, and they serve both expressive and formal purposes. The supposed distinction between the emotional effects of major and minor in modern Western music is a case in point. The distinction rests on a convention, true, but on a convention that developed naturally out of the structure of the tonal system and fulfilled an important expressive need.

A more specific example may make this point clearer. It might be argued that the expressive associations of the Funeral March from Chopin's Sonata in B-flat minor depend on mere convention—on the fact that we recognize the combination of common meter, slow tempo, ponderous beat, and somber color, as adding up to a conventional symbol that reads: Funeral March. But, leaving aside the question of how such a symbol could have been established without the existence of compositions (such as Chopin's!) that are supposed to exemplify it, one can reply that the convention is not an arbitrary one. It arose in response to the demands of a specific kind of occasion for which music served a functional purpose, and hence the same convention can be used artistically to evoke a similar occasion in the imagination. The convention thus places the composition in a musical context that includes, in this case, the demands of a familiar human situation. It is to this situation, and to the (imagined) function that it calls on the music to perform, that the expressive associations of the Chopin movement should be attributed.

The formalist forgets, moreover, that even a purely musical context can be determined by expressive as well as formal factors. When we try to explain the content of one composition in terms of others, we often rely on stylistic resemblances—but not always. Sometimes we find kinship among works that have nothing—at least nothing obvious—in common with respect to technique, form, or style. What they seem to share is a large area of what I have called expressive potential. One's sense of this type of relationship must necessarily be highly subjective, but I suggest as an example Bartok's Sixth Quartet, which I hear as defining an area of content near that of the last quartets of Beethoven. In particular, the fourfold Mesto of the Bartok seems to me close in expressive effect—although neither in idiom nor in structure—to the opening fugue of Beethoven's Op. 131.

The formalist is justified in demanding a purely musical context for music only if he recognizes that (above all for the musician) the musical context and the human context are inextricably intertwined. John O'Hara was right: "Music . . . is to be enjoyed, and we might as well face it: it must have human associations if it is to be enjoyed."[6] In other words: no context, no content. But there is always a context, and there is always a content.

[6] John O'Hara, *Butterfield 8* (New York: Harcourt Brace, 1935), p. 131.

Index